THE TRAITORS

By the same author

•

AFRICAN TRILOGY
comprising
MEDITERRANEAN FRONT
A YEAR OF BATTLE
THE END IN AFRICA

•

ECLIPSE
MONTGOMERY
THE RAGE OF THE VULTURE
THE VILLA DIANA
THE TRAITORS
RUM JUNGLE
GALLIPOLI
A SUMMER NIGHT
THE RUSSIAN REVOLUTION
NO ROOM IN THE ARK
THE WHITE NILE
THE BLUE NILE

THE TRAITORS

by Alan Moorehead

WITH A NEW PREFACE

Harper & Row, Publishers, New York, Evanston, and London

Contents

•

CONTENTS

Illustrations

•

The following will be found after page 94.

Wing Commander Henry Arnold and William James Skardon, security officers at Britain's atomic research station at Harwell

Dr. Nunn May, leaving London by plane after his release from prison

Bruno Pontecorvo

Klaus Fuchs at the time of his arrest

Sir John Cockcroft, director of the Harwell research project

Harry Gold and David Greenglass

Lord Chief Justice Goddard

Preface to New Edition

•

BASICALLY THIS IS A BOOK ABOUT CONSCIENCE, AND I WAS TAKEN TO
task on the matter by several English critics when the first edition
was published eleven years ago. They did not agree with my con-
tention that a man's conscience is not necessarily his best or only
guide—that indeed, in certain circumstances (as in the case of
these three traitors), it could be a very bad and harmful guide.
One anonymous reviewer in *The Listener,* which is a respectable
weekly published by the B.B.C., even went so far as to say that
if I held such views no one could be certain as to which way I
myself might jump if Britain were ever again attacked by a foreign
power. I was not then, nor am I now, convinced by my opponents'
arguments. It still seems to me that a man's conscience is just as
much the result of his environment and training as of his heredity.
An inborn knowledge of what is right and what is wrong is not
automatically given to us at birth: we have to undergo a long
process of instruction and correction before these fundamental
issues become at all clear. The family background, the society
in which we move, the age in which we live, religion and politics
—certainly politics—all these play a part. The boy brought up
in Nazi Germany will have one sort of conscience, and the son of
a Communist in Russia will have another; and the American or

British boy of the same age will grow up with still another view of what is right and what is wrong.

I am not asserting that a true conscience cannot exist, and that it is not a most admirable and honourable thing: I am simply saying that most consciences are prejudiced and ought not to be taken as a final guide. Even so, I would certainly prefer a man to have *some* sort of conscience rather than none at all, and I am absolutely in favour of his acting upon it provided he does not injure his fellow men.

Now the three men we are dealing with here all obeyed their consciences in giving their support to Soviet Russia. I see nothing ethically wrong in that. But the way they gave their support was wrong. They pretended to be loyal to the democracies, they took oaths that they would never divulge the secrets that they were entrusted with, and yet they gave those secrets to the Russians. A man is certainly entitled to change his mind about his political beliefs, but if he does so he is bound, I submit, to declare the fact to the world. He should not keep silent and spy upon his friends.

These three men, Nunn May, Fuchs, and Pontecorvo, were of course in a particularly difficult position. They knew about the atomic bomb and they believed no doubt that they were doing something for the future happiness of the world by imparting what they knew to the Russians. But what arrogance this is. Who gave them the right to take such a momentous decision—a decision that drastically affects all our lives? We did not appoint them as our leaders or representatives. They appointed themselves; they obeyed their consciences and it was irresponsible and criminal behaviour. The only honourable thing for these three men to do when they discovered that they were opposed to the policies of the democracies they served was to resign. They would not have been imprisoned or persecuted. Most probably they would have been found useful work in other scientific fields and that would have been the end of the matter. Instead they chose, with marvellous arrogance, to betray us for our own good.

I hold these views now just as strongly as I did eleven years ago, so I have altered nothing in the following pages that I then wrote on this matter of conscience. However, on so vital a question as this I feel bound to put the other side of the case. It has been best expressed by the following letter, which was recently written to me by one of my critics.

"I think where we fundamentally disagree on this question is in the use of the word conscience. What is conscience? The Oxford Dictionary describes it as the 'faculty of distinguishing between right and wrong,' or as the 'consciousness that one's actions are right or wrong.'

"You say that *The Traitors* is a book basically about conscience; I would say that basically it is a book about faith—faith, the 'belief in a religious doctrine or divine truth.' The word divine is the key. No one I think could question the fact that Fuchs was not out for any personal or immediate gain of any sort. (I am only taking Fuchs as an example here, it may not apply to the others so well.) Quite clearly he was prepared to lose everything he had, including his life, for a cause which he believed in so strongly that for him it was divine. Few people believe in causes this much, very few; if they do they must believe that the end, being the ultimate good, justifies the means.

"The means, in this case, were his betrayal of his oath and of his friends, and looked at from their point of view his hands were indeed dirty. None of us could have wished to be Fuchs, least of all Fuchs himself. To dissemble, how degrading: to lie to your friends and fellow workers, how hateful: to identify yourself with one life and live another, how hideously undermining. The responsibility was dreadful. Yet, to my mind, he took the only decision; believing as he did in marxism, what a personal arrogance and denial of conscience it would have been on his part to withhold the information, and by so doing add perhaps a hundred years on to the life and death struggle in which marxism and capitalism were engaged.

"For most people there is no black, no white; there are no heroes and no villains; conscience can make cowards or heroes of us all and who is to say who is right? The issues are too often played out at a personal level, for profit, for hate, from fear, for causes which by no possible interpretation could be considered as divine. A real question of conscience arises, for instance, in Joseph Conrad's book *Under Western Eyes*, where the young student, having sheltered the anarchist who had thrown the bomb at the Minister of State, then gives him away to the police. And then is accepted by the anarchist's companions, who know nothing of this, as their hero. No question here of anything but treachery: to the anarchists, to the police, and finally to himself.

"But when the great faiths are involved—catholicism, marxism, any religion you like—then you cannot expect to restrict people's belief in their faith, to say 'you can believe as far as this but no further.' You say you are in favour of men acting upon their consciences *provided they do not injure their fellow men*. But who is to take this decision as to whether or not it injures or helps them? They? You?

"Fuchs was bound to action; had he done nothing, had he merely resigned from atomic work, he would have taken the weapon out of the soldier's hands—the soldier who was fighting what he believed to be the righteous war. Could he have felt this to be honourable, or would he not rather have been buying his own honour for the price of all he believed in? Unlucky Fuchs. 'Thank God I am not as other men are,' said the Pharisee. Fuchs must have wished to God he was."

Well, there it is. The reader must decide which of us is right.

Apart from all this, I have not found, in revising the text for this new edition, that any other important changes were required.

Despite all appearances to the contrary, the international scene has altered surprisingly little in the last decade. In the thirties and the forties there was a continuous process of realignment; either by external coercion or by revolution countries changed sides with bewildering suddenness, and one after another the colonies of the great European powers claimed their independence. But by the fifties this process was almost complete; the world was divided into East and West, into Communist states and democracies (with some uncommitted countries on the side), and so it has continued. In general, what we thought of Russia ten years ago still holds good today, and the atomic spy is still a familiar figure in the world.

It may be of some interest, however, to recall the circumstances in which this book was written. In 1950 I read the published evidence in the Fuchs case and was absorbed by it, more particularly perhaps because I had recently been reading Dostoievsky's *Crime and Punishment*. Here, it seemed, was Raskolnikov all over again: the split personality, the desire to hide and the desire to confess, and, ultimately, his intimate trust in the policeman who had come to destroy him. I wrote to Mr. Eade, the then Home Secretary in London, saying that I proposed to write a book about Fuchs provided he (Fuchs) consented, and I asked for permission to see him in Stafford gaol. I proposed a series of four meetings, and said I was quite prepared for officials to be present and to monitor the conversation. Mr. Eade wrote back saying that it was impossible for him to grant this permission since it would create a precedent; if other writers approached him with the same request—and no doubt some of them would want to see ordinary criminals—he would not be in a position to refuse them, and this was undesirable. So far as I was concerned, this was the end of the matter.

Soon afterward, however, the question of the atomic spies became a very lively issue, and it was clear that the implications of the Fuchs case extended far beyond the treason of one man. Pontecorvo disappeared, the Allan Nunn May case was remembered, other arrests of atomic spies followed in the United States, and it was obvious that an extensive spy ring was involved. In Washington it was believed that the British security services were very largely to blame, and the interchange of information about atomic weapons between America and Britain, which had been so full and frank during the war, was stopped. The facts were aired fairly fully in America. In 1951 the United States government issued its pamphlet *Soviet Atomic Espionage,* and Mr. J. Edgar Hoover and others added further evidence from the American point of view. In England, meanwhile, nothing official had been published apart from the reports of the two short trials of Nunn May and Fuchs, and a brief statement made by the Prime Minister, Mr. Attlee, in the House of Commons. In the press at home, as well as in America, the British security services were under fire, and it was felt that the time had come to put their side of the case. I undertook this work, and the present book is the result.

I think, however, that I can honestly claim that this is not a work of propaganda—or at any rate that the propaganda is quite secondary. As the research went forward I found my brief slipping further and further into the background, and I became absorbed in the story of just how these men lived their double lives, how their minds worked, how they did their spying, and how they were eventually tracked down and persuaded to confess. I returned, in short, to my original interest in the crime and punishment aspects of the case, and these, I think, are the permanent issues.

The punishment, or at all events the physical side of it, is over now; since this book was written both Nunn May and Fuchs have emerged from prison, and all three men have taken up new careers abroad, two of them behind the Iron Curtain. Nunn May

was the first to be heard from. He got a full remission on his
ten-year sentence for good behaviour, and was released from
Wakefield prison on December 29, 1952. After a brief flurry of
publicity in the press at that time he dropped out of sight for
eight months. Then in August 1953 it was announced that he had
married a Dr. Hildegarde Broda, who had obtained her medical
degree in Vienna in 1938 and who was then serving as a school
medical officer in Cambridge. At this news there was an attempt
in the Cambridgeshire County Council to get her dismissed from
her employment, but it was defeated. The chairman of the
Council declared that Dr. Broda was "doing her job second to
none," and that they did not want McCarthyism in England.

Soon afterward it became known that Nunn May was working
in the Brooklyn Crystallographic Laboratory in Cambridge, and
there he continued until early in 1962. It was then announced that
he had accepted a position as Professor of Physics in the new
University of Ghana, in West Africa. At no point in all this time
did Nunn May make any public declaration about his politics, but
perhaps it is not altogether without significance that Ghana has
had close and friendly relations with Russia since it obtained its
independence (it was the former British colony known as the
Gold Coast), and in fact a new research reactor is being built
there now by the Russians.

Pontecorvo was the next man to reappear. He bobbed up in
Moscow in March 1955, after four years of silence. An article
written by him appeared in both *Pravda* and *Izvestia,* and in it
he declared that he was working in the Institute of Physical
Problems of the Soviet Academy of Science—an organisation
carrying out research for the development of nuclear energy for
peaceful purposes. He praised the Soviet technical equipment and
said that the conditions under which he worked were "splendid."
He added that his situation in Britain had become "intolerable"
by 1950; he was being subjected there to "systematic blackmail

by the police." A few days later he gave a press conference to about 50 Russian and foreign correspondents in the ballroom of the Czar's former summer palace on the outskirts of Moscow. He was wearing a red tie, and the red ribbon and the silver medal of the Stalin Prize were attached to his buttonhole. Speaking in Italian, which was then translated into Russian and English, he appeared composed and at ease, and he answered questions deliberately but with confidence. He declared that the Western powers since 1954 had decided to prepare for atomic warfare while Russia was committed to peace, and that he was holding this conference because he believed that "a free exchange of opinion would be beneficial."

"I want to address all honest people," he went on, "especially scientists and the citizens with whom I work and whom I respect, and I want them to listen to what I have to say. You cannot stand aside today. The reactionary press in the capitalistic countries is befuddling the minds of many people. There are things which could be understood by children."

The rest of his discourse followed the Party line, but he sent affectionate messages to his family and to his former colleagues in Britain, particularly Professor Cockcroft, and he was able to reveal some interesting things about his private life. He said he had been given the use of a flat in Moscow and of a country house, that his wife and children were with him, that he had been a Soviet citizen for the past three years, and that he had been offered a number of posts in the Soviet Union and had chosen the one he preferred. He was in no way connected with the development of atomic weapons.

Since 1955 Pontecorvo has been mentioned a number of times in the Moscow press, and it is evident that the Russians have recognised his talents as a convivial man. Recently he has been working as a co-ordinator of nuclear research behind the Iron Curtain, and he is chairman of a club of scientists from twelve different Communist countries. It meets at Dubna, near Moscow. He has been recommended for a Lenin prize.

Fuchs too got a remission of his prison sentence for good behaviour. He emerged from Stafford gaol in June 1959, after serving only nine years, and at once flew in a Polish plane to Schönefeld airport in East Germany. Here he was met by his 85-year-old father, with whom he went to live in Leipzig. To journalists who questioned him he said he was still a Marxist, and that he was in the process of becoming an East German citizen. In September 1959 it was announced that he had been appointed Deputy Director of the East German Central Institute for Nuclear Physics at Dresden, where a research reactor was being built with Soviet assistance. At the same time he revealed that he had married Frau Greta Keilson, the widow of the former head of the East Germany Foreign Ministry Press Department. They had first met in Paris when they were both refugees from Nazi Germany.

In 1960 Fuchs was visited by an American journalist in his comfortable villa which overlooks the city of Dresden. He was wearing the East Germany Communist Party badge in his lapel, and said that he had never left the Party but had simply lost touch with it during the war. Looking back on his espionage, he said that he "would do it again." He appeared to be engrossed in his work, which was concerned mostly with the development of industrial atomic energy, and deplored the fact that there was not a fuller exchange of information in this field, especially with America. "With greater industrial power," he added, "we can effectively combat West German militarism."

It will be seen, then, that no great retribution has overtaken any of the three men. They are all married, all living in comfortable circumstances and doing the work they wish to do, and, in the case of Fuchs and Pontecorvo at least, apparently at ease with their consciences again. It may be, of course, that Fuchs and

Pontecorvo were bound to reaffirm their loyalty to Russia in order to obtain and continue with their jobs, and that secretly they have a nostalgia for the West. Perhaps they dream of the day when the West will join hands with Russia to form a common front against China, and thus their private ambivalence will be forgotten and forgiven. But who knows? Perhaps the safest guess is that for the time being they have had enough commotion in their lives and now only wish to continue with their chosen work as private citizens. None of them is young any more. In 1962 Fuchs and Nunn May were 51, and Pontecorvo was 49.

It by no means follows, however, that the cases of these three men put an end to the story of atomic espionage. Almost certainly other unknown spies are at work in the West, other Fuchses, Nunn Mays and Pontecorvos are undetected yet, and part of the object of the republication of this book is to draw attention to that fact. But at least now the security services have had a thorough grounding in the ways of the new type of traitor—the man who is not a professional spy, nor a turncoat politician, nor a man out essentially for personal gain, but a self-appointed idealist who possesses the sort of power that formerly only belonged to governments, and is determined to use it.

Finally, I must express my thanks to my publisher, Mr. Cass Canfield. He thought the book had not received sufficient notice on its first appearance and decided to publish this new edition. I am most grateful to him for this confidence.

ALAN MOOREHEAD

Part One • ALLAN NUNN MAY

One

•

THERE IS NO END TO ESPIONAGE; IT FLOWS ON, IN A PRIVATE WORLD
of its own, through wars and centuries, and clearly we are never
going to know the whole truth about the atomic spies. But just
occasionally some of the truth comes to light, a part of the net
is dragged to the surface, and society is given a brief and forbidding glimpse of what goes on in the secret underworld below.

This happened—or rather it began to happen—in Ottawa in
1945 on the evening of September 5. On that evening a young
cipher clerk in the Russian Embassy named Igor Gouzenko went
to the steel safe in his office and took out a number of official
documents. His job was to encipher and decipher these documents for Colonel Zabotin, the Military Attaché, as they passed
between the Embassy and Moscow, and for some time past he had
been turning down the corners of those which seemed to be of
special interest.

Gouzenko, then 26, was of the generation which has been born
and brought up in Soviet Russia, and he had been just two years
in Canada. But in those two years he had marvelled at the goods
that were sold in the shops, and at the freedom and friendliness
with which the Canadians went about their daily lives, and he
had grown to detest the way in which these people were being
cheated and spied on, when their only desire had been to help

3

Russia in the winning of the war. And now that his term abroad
was over and he was due to return to Russia, he had decided
to put all his past life behind him and cross over to the Canadian
side.

The story of Gouzenko's defection is well known through the
published report of the Canadian Royal Commission which enquired into the matter in the following year, but it is worth
repeating here because of the peculiar atmosphere it evokes, and
because it reveals by how much the democracies were caught
unawares.

It was eight o'clock when he left the Embassy in Charlotte
Street, carrying the documents in his coat pockets, and he went
at once to the offices of the Ottawa *Journal* in the city. He had
the naïve but understandable idea that if he could get his documents published there and then he would have warned the democracies and his purpose would have been accomplished. It was
not, however, so easy as that. Newspapers have settled practices
of their own: crimes, politics, and baseball results come in each
day on an established rhythm, and there is normally no place in
this routine for an earnest foreigner who arrives, without announcement, his pockets stuffed with Russian telegrams, to make
a point-blank exposure of the Soviet Union. Gouzenko argued for
an hour, but could get no one to take him seriously. He then
returned to his home at 511, Somerset Street, where he was living
in an apartment with his wife, Svetliana Borisovna, and their child
Andrei, who had been born since their arrival in Canada.

The next day, September 6, he tried again. He set out with his
family, and his wife carried the documents, a disordered bundle
of pink, blue, and white slips of paper, in her handbag. He returned first to the Ottawa *Journal,* and when they advised him to
go to the police he visited various government offices in the city
with no better result. Mr. Mackenzie King, the Prime Minister,
did indeed hear of this odd visitor just as he was about to go into

an opening session of the Canadian Parliament. But it is not a Prime Minister's business to receive junior clerks from foreign embassies—such a procedure would make friendly international relations impossible—and he advised his staff to send Gouzenko and his documents back to the Russian Embassy—if that, indeed, was where they had come from. The family then returned to their home toward seven in the evening.

By now Gouzenko had every reason to fear the consequences of what he had done. Soon after he got indoors he saw two men standing on the opposite side of the street watching his apartment, which was No. 4. Presently there was a knock at his door, and he heard someone call his name. He recognised the voice of Under-Lieutenant Lavrentiev, one of Colonel Zabotin's drivers from the Embassy. Gouzenko and his wife remained quite still, but the child ran across the room, making it clear they were at home.

Gouzenko then went out onto the balcony at the back of his apartment and called to his neighbours in No. 5, a Canadian Air Force sergeant and his wife. He asked if these two would take care of the child that night in case anything should happen to himself and his wife. The Canadian took him indoors, and Gouzenko then explained that he believed that he was in danger, that the Russians might try to kill him and his wife during the night.

This was the first intimation Gouzenko was able to convey to the outside world of the real difference between the society he was about to leave and the one he was about to enter. In the intervening years since then we have grown used to the idea that the citizens of a police state can be killed, wherever they may be, in the most matter-of-fact way and in the most prosaic surroundings. But in 1945 it was not clear. To most people then it was inconceivable that Russia had already turned against her allies— the war had ended only a few weeks before—and Gouzenko's

story must have sounded very strange to the young Canadian
sergeant and his wife.

It was agreed, however, that the child should be left with them
in No. 5 for the rest of the night. But as the Canadian was letting
Gouzenko out by the back way onto the balcony, they saw a man
walking along a lane at the rear of the building. Gouzenko was
now thoroughly alarmed, and he asked if the whole family could
take refuge with the Canadians. At this point the woman who
lived in apartment No. 6 appeared, and, since she was alone, she
offered to put up the Gouzenkos, while the Air Force sergeant
went off for the police on his bicycle.

While the Gouzenkos were moving into No. 6, two constables,
Walsh and McCulloch, arrived in a prowler car. They heard the
story, and agreed to keep watch on the building through the night;
the bathroom light in No. 6 was to be kept on, and in the event of
an emergency it was to be turned out. Nothing happened for the
next three or four hours. Then, shortly before midnight, four
Russians arrived, and began knocking on the door of Gouzenko's
apartment, No. 4. The Air Force sergeant in No. 5, thinking it was
the police, opened his door, and when the four men asked if he
knew where Gouzenko was, he said he did not know. Despite this,
the men kept knocking on Gouzenko's door for a time. Then at
last they went away, and the Air Force sergeant returned to his
apartment. The four men, however, did not leave the building.
They returned quietly, knocked again at No. 4, and then broke
open the door and went inside.

Meanwhile Walsh and McCulloch in the street outside had got
their signal. They came into the apartment and found that it was
being ransacked. One man, Vitali Pavlov, a second secretary and
consul of the Russian Embassy and the head of the Russian
secret service in Canada, was going through a clothes cupboard.
Another man, in uniform, Lieutenant-Colonel Rogov, an assistant
to Zabotin, was searching another cupboard in a room near the

broken front door. The other two men were Lieutenant Angelov, also on Zabotin's staff, and Alexandre Farafontov, a cipher clerk from the Embassy.

All these events are soberly recorded in the report of the Canadian Royal Commission, and the following account of what then occurred is taken from page 641 of that report.

"Walsh asked what the men were doing there. Pavlov, who did practically all the talking, said they were Russians, and they were looking for papers which belonged to the Russian Embassy; that the owner of the apartment had left town and was in Toronto and they had his permission to go into the apartment and get what they wanted. Walsh remarked that it was funny if they had permission that they had broken the lock to get in, and he picked up from the floor the keeper of the lock and said, 'This does not look as if it has been done with a key. You must have used a bit of pressure to get in and from the marks on the door you did not put them there with your fingers.' Constable McCulloch testified that Pavlov said they had 'lost the key but there was something in there they had to get.' Pavlov then said the premises were Russian property and they could do as they liked. Rogov said the constables had insulted them and Pavlov ordered them out, but the policemen refused to go until their inspector arrived."

In other words, they were in Canada, not in a police state where official violence is accepted and unquestioned. Zabotin and his staff had blundered dreadfully on two counts. They had failed first to do something which was also going to harass the governments of all democracies as a consequence of this night, and that was to guarantee the loyalty of one of their employees, to see what was happening inside his mind and make provision for it. They had blundered on the second count in marching so bald-headedly upon their victim, in being so contemptuous of the vigilance of a democratic society that they took no real precautions to hoodwink the police; Gouzenko was simply one of their own, a delinquent, and they had come to claim him. No doubt there had been consternation about Gouzenko inside the Russian Embassy that day, and their need to catch him was urgent, but now with every move their position became worse.

It was useless for them to protest, as they did to the Canadian Department of External Affairs a day or two later, that Gouzenko had decamped with Embassy money, that the constables had been rude, and that Gouzenko should be arrested as a criminal and handed back to them. The cat was out of the bag, and no one there that night could see where this incident would end.

The inspector arrived. The Russians were allowed to depart. Gouzenko, his wife and child spent the rest of the night in No. 6 under the care of the police. Early in the morning the Russians made one more attempt to enter apartment No. 4; a caller crept into the building, but soon went away again. On the morning of September 7, Gouzenko was taken with his documents to the offices of the Royal Canadian Mounted Police. And now that he had established his good faith by an unpremeditated *coup de théâtre*, society was ready to listen to him, and take him and his family into protective custody.

But even the following year, in 1946, when the Royal Commission had published its findings, and revealed how implacable was the Russian opposition to the West, and how deep and far its spy networks could go, it is doubtful if many people realised the full implications of what was happening. Such names as Alger Hiss were still unknown, and it had not yet become clear that we were entering into a new age of somersaulting ethics, where black could be made into white, where a man could consistently say one thing and mean another, and where all the old-fashioned loyalties could be made to mean nothing at all.

The Canadian spy ring was small fry as spy rings go, and (as has developed from later evidence) it had been hastily put together. It only touched the fringe of a much larger international organisation. But its discovery did start a remarkable chain of events because for the first time it brought out into the open the frightening relationship between the new ethics and the new physics, between the traitor and the atomic bomb. From now on, like the explosive force of the bomb itself, the power of the traitor was enormously magnified—magnified to Faustian proportions, beyond any Götterdämmerung which Hitler might have dreamed of in his bunker in Berlin. The traitors themselves did not see it that way. They did not believe themselves to be anarchists. Many of them acted on what they believed to be the most honourable of motives. But that was the way of it, nevertheless; they mixed their science with their politics, and the result was something which the physicists might call "a critical mass"—an appalling thing, highly explosive.

But in 1945, when the war was just over and we were tired, there was still a long way to go before any great public attention was paid to these things. An immense number of facts had yet to be unearthed. In that same month, September 1945, when Gouzenko walked out of the Russian Embassy in Ottawa, Doctor Klaus Fuchs, some thousands of miles away to the south, drove from Los Alamos to Santa Fe and handed over to a Russian agent the details of the actual bomb itself. Four more years were to pass before he was discovered. In that same September a promising young Italian scientist named Doctor Bruno Pontecorvo was working at the very center of British atomic research at Chalk River in Canada; and five years were to go by, almost to the very day, before he and his family vanished without a trace from the Western world at Helsinki in Finland.

There was a third man, Doctor Allan Nunn May, who on this same night of September 5 had just come back to his home in Montreal from a visit to Chalk River. He was packing up for his return to England the following week. Neither he nor either of the others knew anything about Gouzenko's escape. They had never even heard of him. Yet Gouzenko's evidence, and the investigation which followed it, were going to affect them all in some way and ruin them in the end. And from these men the trail was going to lead on to the Americans Harry Gold, David Greenglass, Julius and Ethel Rosenberg, and many others.

Allan Nunn May stood in the most immediate danger. His name under the code word "Alek" was actually mentioned in the correspondence Gouzenko brought out of the Russian Embassy. Doctor May crossed the Atlantic, still unaware of the fate that was hanging over him, and he settled down with every outward appearance of a placid academic existence as a lecturer in physics at King's College, London. It was there in the following March that a detective inspector from Scotland Yard met Doctor May as he was coming from one of his lectures, and told him he was under arrest.

In some ways Nunn May's case is a prototype for all the rest. He was not only the first of the major atomic spies to be discovered; he also revealed the pattern by which nearly all the others can be recognised. He revealed, in fact, that we were dealing with an entirely new sort of traitor: a man who gave away secrets not for money or for power, or through fear or hatred, or the perverse attraction of the act of spying, or even basically because he believed in a political faith. He betrayed because he found himself in possession of information of the utmost value, and with an Olympian confidence decided that he should pass it on for the good of mankind. He did this although of his own free will he had taken an oath that he would never do it. This was something new in the world, a thousand miles away from the conceptions of derring-do confidential agents and glamorous female spies; and from Judas to Shakespeare's Iago there was no real precedent to explain it. Beyond this—this moral content in their treason, which is always somewhere present in a greater or less degree—it would be foolish to lay down rules about the atomic spies. They all led a double life, but there is nothing particularly new in that, except that they carried it so far and so successfully. For the rest, the three men being discussed in this book—Nunn May, Fuchs, and Pontecorvo—differed extremely in their habits, their backgrounds, and their private domestic lives.

Nationality has nothing much to do with the matter. Nunn May was born in England, Fuchs in Germany, and Pontecorvo in Italy. The actual dates of their births may, however, be important, for they were all born within a year or two of one another at the end of the first decade of this century and did their spying in their early thirties; and so they came under the influence of the same succession of political events, at a special and chaotic moment of European history.

On the other hand, a study of races and religions does not get you very far in making rules about traitors; for Pontecorvo was a Jew, while the other two came from Christian families, and none of them were very religious men. There is nothing perverse in their private lives; they were not drunkards, drug-takers, nor pederasts; nor were they mad. Nunn May and Fuchs happened to be bachelors and were of a retiring disposition; Pontecorvo was married, with three children, and by nature an extrovert. It is true they were all unusually gifted and highly educated men—perhaps too highly in the one direction of physics, for there is not much evidence that they took any lively interest in the humanities. They had no time.

Even in the best of circumstances they would probably never have become friends; in fact, though they met for short periods in different places, they barely knew one another. Almost certainly none of them knew that the others were working for the Russians until the arrests were made: Fuchs, indeed, discussed the May case among his friends—just as later Pontecorvo discussed Fuchs —with an air of genuine surprise (though admittedly this too may have been false).

In following the careers of the three men, it is always necessary to keep the contemporary political events in mind, for there is no real understanding of their treason to be had in any other way. It is futile to look back at them over the gulf of the last World War, and the politics of the 1950's and 1960's can be extremely misleading about the past. One has to approach these men subjectively. Their first memories, as small children, were of war. They were at school in the 1920's, when Europe was painfully trying to recover its equilibrium—the days of inflation, of collapsing governments, of new politics arising out of famine and inequality.

It is true that by the time they entered their universities there was some stability in the world again, but almost at once the economic depression paralyzed the scene, and it is hardly surprising that these three young men, whose lives are almost synchronous with the rise of Marxist socialism, should have begun to look toward the Soviet Republic as the one white hope in an impossible world.

Then, about the time they were taking their degrees and moving on to postgraduate research (Nunn May at Cambridge, Fuchs at Kiel, and Pontecorvo at Rome), the Reichstag in Berlin was burned down, the Nazis began their extermination of the Jews and the Communists, and from that moment (the spring of 1933) events in Europe were precisely calculated to entrench the impressionable left-wing student in the belief that his cause was the true, in fact the only, one. Within six years there followed Mussolini's attack on Abyssinia, the Japanese aggression in China, the Spanish Civil War, the Anschluss, Munich, the German seizure of Prague, and finally the onset of the war itself. Every new disaster seemed to demonstrate that Russia and the left wing had been right since the beginning: the Fascists had to be destroyed. And, in fact, left-wing foreign policy became the foreign policy of democratic governments everywhere. The left wing, in other words, was a popular and entirely legal movement, especially in the universities, and this sometimes forgotten fact has to be remembered in appreciating the three men we are considering here.

I offer this point, not by way of apology for the traitors (tens of thousands of other students were affected by the same events and never turned to treason), but as the background of their conduct and part of the explanation of it. In setting down their case histories in the following pages I have had one main object in view—to try and discover why they acted as they did. I have moved on the general presumption that they are not monsters or freaks who suffered from some disease or aberration in the brain, but rather that they are an extension of society itself, and that they are, in some degree, symptomatic of the times in which we are living. Certainly they were all in a special position. Had they been zoölogists, the chances are that we would never have heard of them, for they would have had no great secrets to betray and the Russians would not have bothered with them. But they were physicists, and they found themselves for a short time in possession of a great secret. They arrived at a point of power almost by accident. They had no training in the use of power. None of them struggled up to it by force of character or through political elections or by virtue of an hereditary position. Power simply fell into their laps.

Ninety-nine per cent of us never have an opportunity of altering history, but these men had that opportunity. They were not professional spies. They were educated men, who, like most of the rest of us, had formed ideas about the political problems of the world, and (unlike the rest of us) were suddenly given an opportunity of taking direct action. Why these men in particular should have turned traitor when the vast majority of their colleagues did not—this surely is a question that has got to be answered if we are going to know the meaning of security ever again, for there will be others like them, subjected to the same temptations. Somehow we have got to discover where men's loyalties really lie and then fix them in their loyalties so that we shall know an enemy from a friend. We have also got to know whether the security services in Britain and North America blundered over these men, and whether some special protection against their kind can be taken in the future, and there is an attempt to answer these questions in this book.

I have not tried to go into the fearfully complicated physics that were the material of these men's treason. On the technical side all we are concerned with here is the administrative system that was set up for the construction of the atomic bomb, and that can be stated simply.

By 1939 scientists all over the world were developing their enquiries into nuclear fission and exchanging information about it. Some of the most distinguished of these men were Germans— and Hitler drove them out because they were Jews. They came to France, Britain, and the United States. As soon as war broke out they began to consider the possibility of converting their discoveries into a new weapon.

At Cambridge, and elsewhere in England, a great deal of work on nuclear physics and related studies had already been done before the war by such men as Sir James Chadwick, Sir John Cockcroft, and other British scientists. They were joined in the 1930's by Peierls, Simon, Born, and others who were forced out of Germany, and in the prewar years England was in some respects ahead of the thinking and experimentation in Germany or anywhere else. During the early part of the war, work on the atomic-energy problem started on only a small scale both in Britain and the United States—most of our nuclear physicists went to work on urgent radar problems.

Rumours reached us early in 1940 about German work on atomic energy. The German scientists of true Aryan stock who had remained in Germany were known to be at work, but there was little information of their progress. So the making of the bomb was to some extent a race in which one never knew whether one was ahead of or behind one's opponent.

As the Nazis moved westward across Europe, the British team was strengthened by the arrival of other refugees, notably two French physicists, Halban and Kowarski, who escaped from France with 165 litres of heavy water which the French government had recently purchased from Norway. Being refugees—many of them enemy aliens—foreign scientists were not at first drawn into the urgent and secret work on radar, but they were free to develop their ideas on the atomic bomb. From 1940 onward, together with their British colleagues they began urging upon the Churchill government a greatly accelerated research programme, even though it might cost—as some of them optimistically estimated—as much as a battleship.

By 1941 matters had reached a point where the independent research in the universities needed to be grouped under one central direction. In great secrecy this directorate was set up in London in October 1941, under Sir Wallace Akers, of Imperial Chemical Industries, and given the deliberately misleading name of "Tube Alloys." Contracts were let out to a number of leading industrial firms for the necessary equipment; special grants were made for research, and, as the results and calculations came in, a steady flow of information began to pass among the laboratories.

Then, toward the end of 1941, two American scientists, G. B. Pegram and H. C. Urey, came to England to exchange ideas; and from this time forward, with many political hitches and hesitations, the British and American efforts marched forward together. Since Britain was under fire, and the United States offered such immense facilities, it was decided to transfer the bulk of the experimental work to North America, and it was during these comparatively early days of the project that Nunn

May and Fuchs were enlisted in England and Pontecorvo in Canada.

In presenting this material I have relied very much upon the help given me by the Atomic Energy Division of the British Ministry of Supply, and by many of the scientists, officials, and others who knew Nunn May, Fuchs, and Pontecorvo at the various stages of their careers. This is in no way an official book —the original idea of it, the pattern, and the opinions expressed are entirely my own. I have tried, however, to give a somewhat fuller and perhaps a fairer picture than has hitherto been presented of the British activity in these cases, and I am indebted to the authorities for allowing officials to check my facts, and, within the limits of official security, to help me where they could.

I have also availed myself of the government documents published in Britain, the United States, and Canada: of transcripts of the court cases, statements in the House of Commons and at Congressional hearings, and of a mass of informed but unofficial material which has appeared in print since these events came to light.

If I do not give the names here of the many people who have helped and encouraged me, it is because there is still much controversy over these matters, and I do not think they should be associated in any way with the opinions and conclusions in this book. They may agree with me, and they may not. The least I can do is not to embarrass them. I can only hope that they know that I remember our meetings with gratitude, and that they will accept my general thanks.

Two

•

EVEN THE PEOPLE WHO KNEW ALLAN NUNN MAY WELL HAVE A
difficulty in describing him precisely, though they make their
meaning clear enough. To some he was a "charming, shy little
man with a dry sense of humour." Others remember him as
"colourless," as "rather a mousy little chap like a suburban bank
clerk," as "very quiet and retiring." At the time of his arrest he
wore glasses, he was going bald, and he affected a small, dark
Hitlerite moustache. He lived alone, very quietly, a senior reader
in physics at King's College, London, on a salary of £800 a year.
When his acquaintances search their memories they can find
little else to say about him (though they still talk for hours
about Fuchs and Pontecorvo). On one thing, however, they are
all agreed—that there was nothing whatever remarkable about
the appearance or the manners of Doctor Nunn May.

He was born on May 2, 1911, at King's Norton, near Birmingham, in Worcestershire, one of a family of one girl and three
boys. His father was a brass founder, and moderately well-to-do.
From the first, Allan Nunn May was an exceptionally hard
worker. At 13 he was a Foundation Scholar at King Edward's
School in Birmingham, and from there scholarships carried him
on to Trinity Hall at Cambridge. His masters at Birmingham
recall that he was a solitary boy, but not gauche in any way,

17

or narrow in his interests; in his written papers he had a very good literary style. It was felt that he might have been just as successful in the humanities as in physics or mathematics. His record at Cambridge was brilliant; in 1931 he had a First Class Mathematics Tripos, and in 1933 he graduated as a Bachelor of Arts and obtained a First Class Natural Sciences Tripos. He stayed on at Cambridge after graduating, one of the most promising young men of his year, and in 1936 he got his doctorate in philosophy. That also was the year when in September he paid a visit to Leningrad.

Nunn May never made any secret of his left-wing sympathies. Few left-wing people did in England in the 1930's. These were the years when the undergraduates at Oxford passed a resolution that under no circumstances would they fight for King and Country. At Cambridge, where Nunn May passed his most impressionable years, there was an even stronger movement toward the left, and it was nothing extraordinary that he should have been drawn into the anti-Fascist movement there. Many others were in it too—men like Donald Maclean and Guy Burgess, who vanished from the British Foreign Office in 1951 and have been in Russia ever since. On logical and humanitarian grounds, if for nothing else, the left wing made an obvious appeal to British undergraduates in the 1930's, when the Russian experiment was still new, and it was bolstered by a sincere and adolescent indignation.

Marxism was a challenge; it required a faith so strong that you had to rise above the normal weaknesses of mankind, and even deny your own family if need be. You were embarked, in fact, on nothing less than the reformation of the world.

The English universities never felt the full shock of the struggle that was going on between the left and the right on the Continent. There were no purges in England, no beatings-up, no castor oil treatment, or internment camps. It was more of

a philosophic than a political approach to Marxism. Yet a kind
of vicarious heat was generated, and the left-wing students soon
found opportunities for direct action.

The midlands of England, where Nunn May was born and
educated, were particularly hit by the economic depression at
the end of the 1920's. Close by in Wales many of the miners
had already been out of work for ten years, and now their plight
became dreadful. It was no very remarkable thing when one
day four unemployed men pooled their last few shillings to hire
an old car and drive it over the sea walls at Bristol, in one final,
futile protest—simply because life was not worth living any more.

At Cambridge some of the students began to make common
cause with the workers. They welcomed the hunger marchers
on their way to London, and fought in street brawls on their
behalf. When Sir Oswald Mosley's black-shirt movement appeared—a pale reflection of the Nazi and Fascist parties on the
Continent—they went to his meetings with the deliberate object
of making trouble. But it was the Spanish Civil War that really
aroused them. Boys of nineteen and twenty at Cambridge and
the other universities abandoned their studies and went off to
fight with the International Brigade in Spain. There were not
many of them, but when they died or became wounded they
were heroes in their day—the first martyrs in the new tradition
of philosophical idealism which was to save the world from
another war.

Allan Nunn May was not a man of action. He slipped through
these events very quietly. He imbibed the philosophy, but he
did nothing drastic to implement it. He never distinguished
himself at political meetings, or in the street brawls; nor did
he go to Spain. Soon after his return from Russia in 1936, however, he became a member of the editorial board of the *Scientific
Worker*, the official journal of the National Association of Scientific Workers, an organisation that included many Communists;

and from this platform and in other ways he continued his unobtrusive, persistent support of the left.

Then the war broke out, and the class struggle was swal-
lowed up in the emergency. Most students and undergraduates
(including most of those who had voted for the Oxford resolution) forgot their politics and went off to fight. Nunn May was
placed on a reserved list as a scientist. Shortly before the war
he had left Cambridge and taken a teaching post at London
University. His department was evacuated to Bristol, and he
lived at Long Ashton, just outside the town. He was recognised
now, at the age of 29, as an exceptional man in his field of
experimental physics—not one of the first flight, but certainly
a man with a promising research career ahead of him—and he
was befriended by such distinguished men as Professor C. F.
Powell, who later won the Nobel Prize for his work in physics.
Then, soon after the war began, he was moved back to London,
where he worked under Sir Charles Ellis.

Here he continued until the spring of 1942. Ellis found him
a precise and imaginative worker, one of the ablest experimen-
talists in the physics laboratory. It was partly on Ellis's recom-
mendation that in April 1942 Nunn May was invited to join
the "Tube Alloys" project in the Cavendish Laboratory at Cambridge—that same laboratory where Nunn May had worked so
well half-a-dozen years before. It was known that in the past
Nunn May had been sympathetic to the left wing in his private
conversations, but there was nothing unusual in this—so, indeed,
had been many other scientists who were now devoting all their
energies to the winning of the war. A pro-Russian man was a
sound anti-Hitler man. In June 1941, Russia had been invaded
by Germany, and she was our strongest—almost our only—ally
in the actual battlefield.

The extreme secrecy of the work at Cambridge was explained
to Nunn May, and it was then that he signed the Official Secrets

Act, which was the same thing as taking an oath that he would never divulge the nature or the details of his duties to an unauthorised person. For the next eight months he was at work in Cambridge, and from all accounts he worked well.

There is no evidence that May was an active member of the Communist Party, or that during these eight months he was in contact with the Russian Intelligence Service. On his arrest in 1946 he refused to identify his contacts, and having made a short statement confirming the facts already known about his treason in Canada, he has refused any further information ever since. It well could be, however, that he did make some contact while he was at Cambridge, for Gouzenko's documents make it clear that the Director of Intelligence in Moscow knew all about him. It was the Director in Moscow who instructed Colonel Zabotin in Ottawa to get in touch with May, and the password was supplied by Moscow. It was "Best regards from Mikel." This makes it clear that May already knew that password, and may have known it for a long time—even when he was still in England.

Outwardly, in 1942 he was immersed in his work, and doing it so well that in January 1943 he was asked to go to Canada as a senior member of the British team working with the Canadians in Montreal. This organisation was a joint Anglo-Canadian effort, for by now it was realised that with Britain under extreme pressure in the war a great deal of the experimental effort could be more profitably done on the other side of the Atlantic. In Montreal, too, the British could maintain a closer co-operation with the Americans, besides advancing their own heavy-water project in conditions of security and safety. Chalk River, an isolated spot in the open country to the west of Ottawa, was later chosen as the site for the larger heavy-water pile. For the next two and a half years, while the bomb was perfected and the war won, May moved regularly between Chalk River and Montreal, and paid some visits to the Argonne Laboratory in Chicago.

He travelled to Canada in January 1943, on a banana boat, with half-a-dozen colleagues and their wives. He was the only British-born scientist in the party and the senior member of it. Looking back now on that crossing, some of the members of the party recall that May was neither very convivial nor noticeably detached. As usual, he was simply quietly there, in the background, volunteering nothing, but willing to be drawn into any activity. One night they played the game of murders. It was a difficult matter for the player who had to find the murderer among the paraphernalia on the blacked-out decks. One of the wives remembers that when it came to her turn to be the detective, she saw May standing there, mildly supercilious, and apparently aloof from the game. She dismissed him from her mind and went off in search of the others. It was May who turned out to be the murderer.

In Canada he lived sometimes in staff messes, sometimes sharing an apartment, and sometimes alone. Toward the end he had an apartment on Swail Avenue in Montreal. He was the one whom the wives of the other scientists asked to dinner—not out of any special friendship, but because they thought he was so much alone, and they were sorry for him. But life for Allan Nunn May blossomed out considerably in Canada. He had more money to spend. The drab, blacked-out cities of England were now replaced by lighted streets, and by the reassurance that comes from warmth, good food, and physical safety. Despite his reputation of being a lonely figure, he did make attachments, and it is possible that he began to discover an affection and a confidence that had been lacking in his life before. In other words, the same stimuli in Canada that drew Gouzenko over to the side of the Western democracies were working in precisely the opposite way in the case of Nunn May. He has never revealed, as Fuchs has, the secret processes of his mind, and the circumstances which led him to become a traitor. But he did have this comfortable and assured position through the last half of the war, and his friends believe that this had a bearing on his decision to pass information to the Russians. It was the gesture of a man who has got something to spare, of one who has to prove himself a hero in the midst of comfort.

Nunn May was an experimental physicist, and his work was concerned with the wider aspects of atomic research rather than with the bomb itself. Nevertheless, he knew about some of the steps that were leading up to the construction of the bomb; he knew about the graphite piles at Hanford, and the production of plutonium, and he was fully conversant with all that was being done in Montreal, and at the heavy-water pile at Chalk River. He made four separate visits to Chicago in 1944, and General Leslie R. Groves, who was the military commander of the American atomic research organisation, has recorded in a letter to Senator Hickenlooper what the Americans knew of him. In this letter, dated March 12, 1946, Groves says:

He had been investigated, for security purposes, by the British Intelligence. That organization cleared him for access to any atomic energy work. It was not practicable nor was it our custom to look behind the approval of the British organization as to the trustworthiness of any individual whom they had investigated. I am sure that they found no indication that he was not completely loyal and of unquestioned integrity.

The General goes on to relate the details of May's visits to Chicago, and he adds:

By this time [October 1944] May had spent more time and acquired more knowledge at the Argonne than any other British physicist. Although I had absolutely no reason to suspect him, I did not like to have him acquire such a wide knowledge of later developments. It is for that reason that in the spring of 1945 I declined to approve a proposed fourth visit of one month's duration. May never returned to the Chicago Laboratory and never visited any other Manhattan District installation.*

There is an obvious contradiction here. General Groves is in effect saying: "We accept the British clearance of these men: on the other hand we do not trust them."

General Groves was of course in a difficult position. The Americans wanted the help of the British, but the British were after all foreigners. The Americans had no means by which they could readily investigate the scientists who were sent to them— even if it had been politic for them to do so. They had to take the British clearance on trust. Yet the fact is that some sort of investigation *was* necessary, since all the atomic traitors, both British and American, were for a long time in America, and the great bulk of their spying was done there. It is one of the unhappy objects of this book to prove that all security is inevitably fallible, particularly in the case of the atomic spies, and on both sides of the Atlantic.

This is a point we can return to later on. All we need note here is that the American misgivings about the British—misgivings that were justified, as it has turned out—had a strong bearing on the mind of Allan Nunn May, for as soon as you keep a secret from your friends you breed a mystery, and even though you have the best intentions in the world, that mystery breeds distrust.

Nobody likes to be kept in the dark. And it is a fact that the British scientists in Canada did feel they were being kept in the dark—especially in the early days of the project, when they hung about idly in Montreal, waiting for equipment and supplies of heavy water with which to carry on their experiments. It would be foolish to pretend that there has been a full inter-

* "Manhattan Engineer District" was the name given for the atomic research organisation in the U.S.A.

change of information between the Americans and the British. There has been scientific collaboration on a scale never attempted before between two nations, but it stops short of a full exchange. By how much more, then, did the Americans stop short in their relations with Russia. To a man like Nunn May, a self-appointed world saver, this was a galling thing. It was not right. The Russians were our allies, and in this important matter he considered that they should have been taken into our confidence. He chose, through some peculiar logic of his own, to overlook the fact that the Russians themselves were the worst of collaborators—inconceivably more suspicious than the Americans. Throughout the war they confided practically nothing to their Western allies. But Russia had a special sanctity in the eyes of Nunn May; perhaps the hope of the world lay with them after the war. And so he decided to present them with his small mite of knowledge, acquired and stolen, in order to redress their ignorance.

The methods by which Nunn May proceeded to his espionage are fairly well known from the documents which Gouzenko brought out of the Russian Embassy in Ottawa and from the evidence of Gouzenko himself. Certainly by the spring of 1945 his contact with the Russians was established—that vital spring when the first atomic bomb was about to be tried out in the Alamogordo desert, and the Russian Intelligence Service was pulling every possible wire to obtain advance knowledge of it. The Director in Moscow first suggested to Colonel Zabotin in Ottawa that May should be approached through Fred Rose, the Communist member of Parliament who was one of the central figures in the Canadian net. Zabotin, however, thought this too obvious, and therefore too dangerous. He asked and got permission from Moscow to use one of his own men, Lieutenant Pavel N. Angelov, to make the contact. This Angelov was the same man who, with three other Russians, later broke into Gouzenko's apartment. It is always the practise of the Russian Intelligence Service to disguise their agents' real names, even inside the network, and Angelov was given the code name "Baxter." Nunn May became "Alek." By some means—not now known—Moscow got in touch with "Alek," and warned him that "Baxter" would approach him, giving the password "Best regards from Mikel."

At this stage Nunn May was directed by the Russians primarily toward obtaining information about uranium and atomic energy rather than about the bomb. Through the spring and early summer there may have been one or more meetings with "Baxter," at which "Alek" handed over all the information in his possession about atomic research in Canada and the U.S.A. This information was sent by cable to Moscow, while "Alek"'s own handwritten notes followed on by bag. For these services "Baxter," early in April 1945, gave Nunn May $200. The notes were stuffed into a whisky bottle, presumably for the sake of secrecy; meetings between spies usually took place in the street.

A second—genuine—bottle of whisky was apparently given to May at the same time. "Baxter," on his return to the Embassy, made a note of the transaction: "200 dollars ALEK and two bottles of whisky handed over 12.4.45."

Then, sometime in July, "Alek" warned the Russians that his job in Canada was coming to an end and that he must soon return to London. Zabotin wired Moscow for instructions, and in a telegram dated July 28, 1945, the Director replied:

Try to get from him ["Alek"] before departure detailed information on the progress of the work on uranium. Discuss with him: does he think it expedient for our undertaking to stay on the spot; will he be able to do that or is it more useful for him and necessary to depart for London?

Contact with Nunn May was made again in the first week of August, and this turned out to be for the Russians perhaps the most fruitful meeting of all, for Nunn May had succeeded in stealing—probably from the laboratories in Montreal—minute samples of separated uranium isotopes. By now the first atomic bombs had been dropped, and "Alek" was able to report on this too; no doubt he got his information through some grapevine of the scientists. The samples, together with May's written report, were regarded as so important that a Colonel Motinov, the Assistant Russian Military Attaché in Ottawa, was instructed to fly with them at once to Moscow. They were placed in a container marked by May "2½" or "250" "enriched." At the same time the following telegram was sent:

To the Director.
Facts given by Alek: (1) the test of the atomic bomb was conducted in New Mexico [with "49," "94–239"]. The bomb dropped on Japan was made of uranium 235. It is known that the output of uranium 235 amounts to 400 grams daily at the magnetic separation plant at Clinton. The output of "49" is probably two times greater (some graphite units are planned for 250 mega watts. i.e. 250 grams each day). The scientific research work in this field is scheduled to be published, but without the technical details. The Americans already have published a book on this subject.*
Alek handed over to us a platinum with 162 micrograms of uranium 233 in the form of oxide in a thin lamina. We have had no news about the mail.

The telegram was signed "Grant," which was Zabotin's code name. Zabotin was also able to send some further details which May had supplied him, about the American electronically controlled antiaircraft shells which were then being used against the Japanese suicide fliers. Finally, on this most successful day, the Russians got a report from May on another Englishman, Norman Veall, whom they were thinking of employing. May went to some length in advising them about Veall. Though Veall

* This was the H. D. Smyth report, published by the U. S. Government in August 1945. It was the fullest account yet given on how the bomb was made.

was a junior man and some eight years younger, May knew him well. They had met at Cambridge, at meetings of the Association of Scientific Workers, and for some time May had tutored Veall for a degree in physics. For this purpose he had visited Veall at his home every week. Veall was a member of a party of British scientists that crossed the Atlantic to Canada on another ship at the same time as May, and in Montreal the two men renewed their acquaintance.

Veall later gave evidence to the Canadian Royal Commission, and in the course of it he said that he was a member of the Young Communist League. "I knew quite a few Communists in Cambridge," he added, "and one or two at least were close friends of mine and continued to work in the same lab."

Veall was much too open in airing his political views for May's liking, and in Canada May warned him about it. For obvious reasons, May himself had grown cautious about discussing politics in Montreal, and it was a settled rule of the Russian Intelligence Service that agents should have no open connection with the Communist Party. Veall, moreover, had compromised himself by carrying Communist documents about with him, and he had openly visited the Russian Embassy in Ottawa—another thing that was strictly forbidden to agents or prospective agents. So now, in August 1945, when May was asked his opinion of Veall's usefulness, he was very precise. Veall, he said, occupied a fairly low position, and knew very little. He was also inclined to be careless; as an example of this May pointed out that on one occasion Veall began a conversation with him while Veall's wife was still in the room. Worse still, he was known in the laboratory in Montreal to be a "red."

As a result of this, the Russians decided not to employ Veall, and the network was warned against him. There is no evidence that Veall gave information to the Russians at any time, and the Commission exonerated him with the words: "Veall did not communicate information with respect to atomic work for the reason that the Russians designedly did not ask him."

But from this time forward Zabotin had need of any reliable agent, for the Director began pressing him for more details. Zabotin himself made a journey to the vicinity of Chalk River so that he could make a personal inspection of the exterior of the plant; he urged his men to obtain every fact they could get hold of, and on August 31 he cabled a little fretfully to the Director, who was not an exceptionally grateful master:

> I beg you to inform me to what extent have Alek's materials on the question of uranium satisfied you and our scientists (his reports on production, etc.). This is necessary for us to know in order that we may be able to set forth a number of tasks on this question to other clients.

May himself, having supplied his samples, went off on a visit to Chalk River. He was there on August 16, and it was probably some time before this that he made it clear to the Russians that there was no question of his remaining in Canada: he had to return to England, where a post was awaiting him at King's College, London. It was therefore necessary for careful arrangements to be made so that May could have a contact again in England, in the event of his continuing to have access to useful information there. These arrangements were worked out with London, Ottawa, and Moscow. Already several messages on this subject had passed through Gouzenko's hands at the Embassy. They were from the Director to Zabotin:

> Work out and telegraph arrangements for the meeting and the password of Alek with our man in London.

To this Zabotin had replied at the end of July:

> To the Director:
> We have worked out the conditions of a meeting with Alek in London. Alek will work in King's College, Strand. It will be possible to find him there through the telephone book.

Meetings: October 7.17.27.* on the street in front of the British Museum. The time, 11 o'clock in the evening. Identification sign— Best regards to Mikel. He cannot remain in Canada. At the beginning of September he must fly to London. Before his departure he will go to the uranium plant in the Petawawa district where he will be for about two weeks. He promised, if possible, to meet us before his departure. He said that he must come next year for a month to Canada. We handed over 500 dollars to him.

Moscow then got in touch with their London agents, who evidently suggested an alteration of the arrangements. On August 22, 1945, the Director cabled Zabotin:

The arrangements worked out for the meeting are not satisfactory. I am informing you of new ones.

1. Place: In front of the British Museum in London, on Great Russell Street, at the opposite side of the street, about Museum Street, from the side of Tottenham Court Road repeat Tottenham Court Road, the contact man from the opposite side—Southampton Row.

2. Time: As indicated by you, however, it would be more expedient to carry out the meeting at 20 o'clock, if it should be convenient to Alek, as at 23 o'clock it is too dark.† As for the time, agree about it with Alek and communicate it to me. In case the meeting should not take place in October, the time and day will be repeated in the following months.

3. The password: The contact man: "What is the shortest way to the Strand?"

Alek: "Well, come along. I am going that way."

In the beginning of the business conversation Alek says: "Best regards from Mikel."

Report on transmitting the conditions to Alek.

No doubt these details were communicated to May. He made

---

* Meaning on October 7 or 17 or 27.
† In 1945 there was still a partial blackout of street lamps in London.

a final visit to Chalk River on September 3, and a few days later set off for England. He arrived on September 17, and shortly afterward took up his appointment at King's College in London, where his work was no longer concerned with secret material. But whether he had the desire and the power to do still more harm was no longer of any consequence. For by now Gouzenko had decamped from the Russian Embassy in Ottawa, and Canadian Intelligence officers had already translated the Russian telegrams quoted above. Allan Nunn May's espionage was finished, at least for a decade—and probably forever.

Three

•

IN THE WORK OF COUNTERESPIONAGE THE FIRST OBJECT IS NOT
always to obtain the arrest of spies; indeed, there are often
considerable advantages in allowing the spy to go free—so that
you may observe him at leisure and learn not only the methods
by which he works but the identity of his other contacts as
well. This is a particularly profitable game if you are reasonably
sure that the spy no longer has access to information of importance. And it is a point about which the spies themselves,
of course, are perfectly aware. Hence the elaborate and often
theatrical precautions taken by the Russian agents over their
meetings. At no time could any of them have been certain that
they had not been discovered already and were being watched.

There is one other aspect. Counterespionage is often forced to
work on half-truths, suppositions, implications, and even guess-
work. Often it may pick up half the links in a chain and never
unearth the rest. You may be left with the logical certainty that
a man is guilty, but the evidence available would not stand
up in a court of law and so a conviction could not be obtained.
Then, too, it may often happen that counterespionage officers
will not wish to reveal their evidence publicly, lest they prejudice
other cases they are investigating—lest in catching a mackerel
they miss the shark.

These matters were admirably discussed by Mr. J. Edgar
Hoover, the head of the F.B.I., when he appeared before the
Senate Appropriations Subcommittee in Washington in February
1950. He said:

In a criminal case the identification and arrest of the wrong-doer
are the ultimate objectives. In an espionage case the identification of
the wrong-doer is only the first step. What is more important is to
ascertain his contacts, his objectives, his sources of information and
his methods of communication. Arrest and public disclosure are steps
to be taken only as a matter of last resort. It is better to know who
these people are and what they are doing, and to immobilize their
efforts, than it is to expose them publicly and then go through the
tireless efforts of identifying their successors.

Consequently the Special Branch at Scotland Yard did not
proceed to the interrogation and arrest of Allan Nunn May directly they had word from Canada that his name was mentioned
in Gouzenko's documents. Quite clearly it was of great interest
to learn whether Nunn May was going to keep his appointment
on either the 7th, 17th, or 27th of October, and if not in October
then in November or December. It was important, too, to learn
the identity of the man he was supposed to meet. It was to be
presumed, of course, that as soon as Gouzenko defected, the
Russians had made a rapid check on the documents he had
taken, and had warned their agents accordingly.

Still one could never be sure.

Great Russell Street, the place of the rendezvous, is a fairly
busy street in the center of London. It is dominated by the long
façade of the British Museum, and the other buildings for the
most part are tenanted by respectable publishers. The front of
the Museum is an easy place to watch, for it is an open place,
with no shops fronting the pavement, no great crowds at eight
o'clock at night, and can be easily observed from the windows
on the opposite side of the street.

But Nunn May kept none of the alternative appointments in October; nor did he appear in November. Moreover, there was nothing in his comings and goings at King's College to excite the slightest suspicion. He gave his lectures in physics there in the usual way, and conducted himself with every appearance of being a normal member of the staff of the University. He took rooms at Stafford Terrace in Kensington, saw few friends, and lived very quietly.

It seems possible, therefore, that May had been warned by the Russians. He could not have learned by any legal means of Gouzenko's defection, or of the investigations then going on in Canada, for nothing was released to the press until February 15, 1946, when Mr. Mackenzie King made a public statement in which he announced that a Royal Commission was being set up to investigate the communication of secret and confidential information to a foreign power.

Up to the time of this announcement, Mr. King had had a puzzling and difficult five months. In the previous September, directly he was convinced of the seriousness of the matter, he had visited Mr. Truman in Washington, and had then gone on to England to see Mr. Attlee. He arrived at Southampton on October 6, the eve of Nunn May's first alternative rendezvous outside the British Museum. May's identity had by then been definitely established, and both May himself and the place of rendezvous were watched.

Meanwhile, Mr. Attlee and Mr. King proceeded to the wider aspects of the case, and they were very serious indeed. The Moscow Conference of the winter of 1945 was impending. The foreign ministers of all the major United Nations powers would be attending, and there did seem to be some hope that, negotiating on their own ground, the Russians could at last be brought to an international settlement. Neither Mr. Truman nor Mr. Attlee was at all eager to bedevil the atmosphere of the

conference before it had even started—and that most certainly
would have happened if Mr. King had come out with a denun-
ciation of the Russian Embassy's activities in Ottawa. In any case,
many weeks yet were required by the Canadian police before
they could translate and disentangle Gouzenko's documents—
there were about 100 of them—and identify all the agents who
were mentioned under code names. So it was resolved that Mr.
King should keep silent.

In the winter, however, events pressed upon him. The Moscow Conference ended fruitlessly. In December Colonel Zabotin
vanished. He left Ottawa without informing the Canadian Government, to which he was accredited, and boarded the Soviet
ship SS *Alexander Suvorov* in New York. The ship sailed
clandestinely, by night, without complying with the port regulations. There has been an unconfirmed press report from Russia
that he died of heart failure on arrival there, and he has never
been heard of since. About the same time, various members of
Zabotin's staff—notably Lieutenant Colonel Motinov, the assistant
military attaché, Rogov, and Nunn May's contact, Angelov—also
disappeared. Finally, the Russian Ambassador himself, G. N.
Larubin, left for Russia "on a routine visit," and never returned.
Manifestly, some sort of commotion was going on inside the
Russian Intelligence Service (its Director was another man who
disappeared), and it needed no very great powers of deduction
to realise that by now the Russians were well aware that the
Canadians were making use of the documents, and that the
hunt was on.

By February nothing more had been discovered about Nunn
May, but in Canada the police were ready to proceed to the
arrest of the other suspects whom they had been watching for
months past. Matters then went forward in their inevitable
order. On February 3 the American journalist Mr. Drew Pearson
released in a broadcast the information that a spy ring had been

operating in Canada; on February 5 the order for a Royal Commission was signed; on February 15 Mr. King made his statement, and the police in Canada and England struck together. In Canada thirteen arrests were made. In London, May was for the first time interrogated directly. Commander Burt saw him at Shell-Mex House. From the first, and throughout the subsequent interrogations, May was composed, logical, and apparently unafraid. Burt asked him if he was aware that there had been a leakage of information in Canada relating to atomic energy. He replied that this was the first he had heard of it. When Burt mentioned the names of Zabotin, Angelov, and "Baxter," he said they meant nothing to him, and he denied that he had been approached by any unauthorised person in Canada, or that he had given any secret information. Burt then asked him if, as a British subject, he was not prepared to give the authorities all the help he could. To this May's reply was, "Not if it be counter-espionage." When he was asked to explain what he meant, he said he would not want to give any information that would implicate his friends.

On this the interview closed. Something, at least, had been gained, for here was a tacit admission that information was being held back and that May was in a position to implicate his friends if he chose. Burt went back to him again on February 20. In the intervening five days a close watch had been kept on May, and new information about him had come in from Canada. This time he was confronted directly with the fact that he was known to have had contact with the Russians in Canada and that an appointment had been made for him on his return to London. Burt did not give him all the information that had been gathered on his case, but enough to make it apparent to May that the game was up. At last he broke down, and said: "No, I did not keep that appointment, as when I returned I decided to wash my hands of the whole business." He still refused to identify his contacts; he still took a stand upon the rightness of what he had done, but he dictated this written confession:

About a year ago, whilst in Canada, I was contacted by an individual whose identity I decline to divulge. He called on me at my private apartment in Swail Avenue, Montreal. He apparently knew I was employed by the Montreal laboratory and he sought information from me concerning atomic research.

I gave and had given very careful consideration to correctness of making sure that development of atomic energy was not confined to U.S.A. I took the very painful decision that it was necessary to convey general information on atomic energy and make sure it was taken seriously. For this reason I decided to entertain a proposition made to me by the individual who called on me.

After this preliminary meeting I met the individual on several subsequent occasions whilst in Canada. He made specific requests for information which were just nonsense to me—I mean by this that they were difficult for me to comprehend. But he did request samples of uranium from me and information generally on atomic energy.

At one meeting I gave the man microscopic amounts of U233 and U235 (one of each). The U235 was a slightly enriched sample and was in a small glass tube and consisted of about a milligram of oxide. The U233 was about a tenth of a milligram and was a very thin deposit on a platinum foil and was wrapped in a piece of paper.

I also gave the man a written report on atomic research as known to me. This information was mostly of a character which has since been published or is about to be published.

The man also asked me for information about the US electronically controlled AA shells. I knew very little about these and so could give only very little information.

He also asked me for introductions to people employed in the laboratory including a man named Veall but I advised him against contacting him.

The man gave me [here the phrase "200 Anm" was crossed out] some dollars (I forget how many) in a bottle of whisky and I accepted these against my will.

Before I left Canada it was arranged that on my return to London I was to keep an appointment with somebody I did not know. I was given precise details as to making contact but I forget them now. I did not keep the appointment because I had decided that this clandestine procedure was no longer appropriate in view of the official release of information and the possibility of satisfactory international control of atomic energy.

The whole affair was extremely painful to me and I only embarked on it because I felt this was a contribution I could make to the safety of mankind. I certainly did not do it for gain.

On March 4, 1946, May was arrested. Detective Inspector William Whitehead of the Special Branch went to King's College and at 3.30 p.m. met May as he was coming out of a lecture. The inspector, who did not want to make the arrest inside the college, said to May: "I have in my possession the warrant for your arrest, which I will read to you in a moment," and he asked May to step outside into the street. May got into the police car which was standing there, and Whitehead read him the warrant. He made no comment. He was taken to Bow Street, and charged under the Official Secrets Act, but again made no comment. Indeed, he has made no comment since.

Meanwhile the storm had broken. Mackenzie King's statement, which indicated that many others besides May were implicated, had given the public a first intriguing view of a new landscape in treason, where the mystery of the bomb was added to the mystery of the spy, and it had opened up a new and sinister relationship between Soviet Russia and the countries of the West.

On February 20, while May was being questioned in London, Solomon Lozovski, the Deputy Commissar of Foreign Affairs in Moscow, sent for Leon Mayrand, the Chargé d'Affaires at the Canadian Embassy, and read to him this statement:

The Soviet Government [it said] considers it necessary to make the following statement:

"Soviet organisations have become aware that in the latter periods of the war certain members of the staff of the Soviet Military Attaché in Canada received, from Canadian nationals with whom they were acquainted, certain information of a secret character which did not, however, present great interest for the Soviet organisations. It has transpired that this information referred to technical data of which the Soviet organisations had no need in view of more advanced technical attainment in the U.S.S.R.: the information could be found in published works on radio location, etc., and also in the well-known brochure of the American, H. D. Smyth, *Atomic Energy.*

"It would therefore be ridiculous to affirm that delivery of insignificant secret data of this kind could create any threat to the security of Canada.

"Nonetheless, as soon as the Soviet Government became aware of the above-mentioned acts of certain members of the staff of the Military Attaché in Canada, the Soviet Military Attaché, in view of the inadmissability of acts of members of his staff in question, was recalled from Canada. On the other hand it must be borne in mind that the Soviet Ambassador and other members of the staff of the Soviet Embassy in Canada had no connection with this."

The statement went on to accuse the Canadian press and Government of deliberately making bad blood between the two countries.

The last point in the statement quoted above was probably true, inasmuch as Zabotin, we know, reported direct to the Director of the R.I.S. in Moscow, and according to Gouzenko he used his own code, which was not known to the Ambassador. What was not true, however, was that the information given by the Canadian net, especially by Nunn May, was either insignificant or available in officially published pamphlets.

Nunn May's information went a long way beyond what has appeared in the Smyth report: it went further than anything that has been published even now. Far from its being of no great interest to the Russians, the Director in Moscow was—as we have seen—intensely anxious to get it. Nevertheless, May

did not tell the Russians how to make the atomic bomb; no one
in Canada had that information. That secret was known only
to a very few people in Washington and at Los Alamos in New
Mexico, and May had no access to any documents from them.

The Nunn May trial in London attracted no very great interest—or, at any rate, no very great public indignation. At that
time—so soon after the cease-fire—the public mind was much
more concerned with a different sort of traitor, men like William
Joyce, who had worked for the Nazis in Berlin during the war.
In France, Italy, Holland, and Belgium it was the Nazi collaborationist who was being hunted down in 1946, not the man
who had gone beyond his duty in giving assistance to our allies
the Russians. Even for the more politically conscious people—
who saw that the war with the Germans was dead and done
with, and that a new alignment was taking its place, the East
against the West—this was no moment to provoke an outcry
against Russia. What we wanted was to collaborate with Russia,
to achieve some basis of mutual understanding, and, at all costs,
to avoid another war. Another war was unthinkable. We wanted,
in Wendell Willkie's phrase, one world.

Very many of the scientists who had worked on the atomic
bomb came forward and proposed that while there was still
time, while this awful weapon was still undeveloped, we should
legally do what Allan Nunn May had already illegally done in
his own small way—pass information to the Russians so that
we could arrive at some reasonable arrangement with them.
Through its spokesmen at the United Nations, Mr. Bernard
Baruch and others, the United States proposed the outlawing of
the bomb. It was a handsome offer. The United States was ready
to give up its lead in atomic weapons, to demolish its stockpile,
and turn over its laboratories to the peaceful development of
atomic energy—provided only that Russia on her side would
guarantee to do the same thing. To sane men it seemed incon-

ceivable that Russia, who had suffered so much, could fail to agree. Somehow, in some way, Russia's suspicions, it was felt, could be overcome, and she could be got to see that the West was sincere. This may seem naïve at the present time, but it was not considered so then, and so a spy like Nunn May, a Russian collaborationist, was not outrageously at odds with the current political thinking. In a strange, underhand way he was a guarantee to the Russians that there were men in the West who were on their side, who wanted them to be equals in a free world—as long as there was peace.

This, of course, is putting the most charitable interpretation possible on Nunn May's actions: it is accepting his confession at its face value since it does not take into account that he was a Communist and therefore must have wanted to see the Russian, not the democratic, way of thinking dominate the world. He wanted, presumably, not just one world, but one Russian or Communist world. And as a Communist he must have been prepared to see the destruction of the institutions of democracy in order to get it.

But then, he was an intelligent man—just the sort of man, it was thought, who could be brought around to some rational plan for the security of the world. He did not look like an anarchist. He was as mild as Einstein, as serious as Mr. Baruch. He was a university lecturer and that was where the scandal lay: that a university man could ever have got himself mixed up in this business. He was not very high up in the hierarchy of physicists, it was true; nevertheless, he was an able man, and the representative of a great institution. It was deplorable that he should appear in a police court; something had gone wrong somewhere, and perhaps he was telling nothing less than the truth when he said: "When I returned I decided to wash my hands of the whole business. . . . The whole affair was extremely painful to me and I only embarked on it because I felt this was a contribution I could make to the safety of mankind." In other words, he was claiming that he had acted on the best of motives, and he could not bring himself to admit that he had really done wrong in the larger moral hemispheres of thinking—in which, apparently, he lived. This was the stand on which his counsel based his case in court.

There were two police-court hearings and a trial, each conducted with dispatch, and—since so much was still secret—with the minimum of evidence. He first appeared at Bow Street on March 5, 1946, and was remanded for a fortnight while the prosecution gathered further evidence. On March 20 he was brought again before the court at Bow Street, pleaded not guilty, and reserved his defence. Having heard a brief account of his career, his confession, and the circumstances of his arrest, the magistrate committed him for trial at the Old Bailey. Bail was refused.

The Old Bailey trial, on May 1, 1946, was a full-dress affair before Mr. Justice Oliver, with the Attorney General, Sir Hartley Shawcross, prosecuting and Mr. Gerald Gardiner appearing on behalf of the prisoner. The proceedings opened with:

The clerk of the court: "Allan Nunn May, you are charged with communicating information contrary to the Official Secrets Act, 1911, and the particulars are that on a day between the 1st of January and the 30th of September, 1945, for a purpose prejudicial to the safety and interest of the State you communicated to a person unknown information which was calculated to be or might be useful to an enemy. Are you guilty or not guilty?"

The prisoner: "Guilty, my Lord."

Sir Hartley Shawcross began by describing this as "a somewhat squalid case" of a man who had set himself up above the laws and the policy of his country—though it was true that there were people who thought that the atomic discoveries should be shared among all nations. Indeed, this was a hope to which we must aim—that the United Nations Organization would be able to establish conditions of sufficient confidence and stability to make that course possible.

Nunn May had signed the Official Secrets Act. He had known what he was doing. Yet he had given information, and accepted money for it. May's confession was read out in full, except for the reference to the samples of uranium—those details were still judged secret at the time.

Mr. Gardiner, in defending, admitted at once that the agent to whom May had given information was a Russian. He said that May had not given away the actual secret of the bomb; his information had merely saved foreign scientists engaged on atomic energy research a certain amount of time. Mr. Gardiner went on:

Doctors take the view, rightly or wrongly, that if they have discovered something of benefit to mankind, they are under an obligation to see that it is used for mankind and not kept for any particular group of people, and there are scientists who take substantially the same view.

May, in doing what he did, had not worked in concert with any other British scientists—he had come to this decision entirely on his own responsibility, and without reference to anyone else. In February 1945—when the acts were committed—the British Army was mostly in Holland, certainly not across the Rhine, and the Russians were in the course of their drive to Berlin. It was customary to refer to them as allies, who were doing at least their fair share in the war. It was perhaps an ironical expression if anyone at that date referred to them as enemies or potential enemies.

At this point the Attorney General interjected:

My Lord, I think I ought to make it abundantly clear that there is no kind of suggestion that the Russians are enemies or potential enemies. The Court has already decided that this offence consists in the communication of information to unauthorised persons—it might be to your lordship, it might be to me or to anyone. . . . What is hit at by this section is the fact that once information passes out of the control of His Majesty's Government, although in the first instance it may be to persons whose attitude to this country is entirely friendly, there no longer remains control over it and it may get into the hands of enemies.

Mr. Gardiner then returned to his point that May had been influenced by a statement made by Mr. Churchill to the effect that we had offered Russia any technical or economic knowledge in our power which was likely to be of assistance to her. Rightly or wrongly, May felt full of indignation that the promises of communication of technical assistance that had been given to one ally should have been made the monopoly of another.

Mr. Gardiner concluded:

He had nothing to gain, except what we all have to gain by doing what we believe to be right; and he had everything to lose.

May was asked if he had anything to say, and he answered, "No, my Lord."

This was Mr. Justice Oliver's sentence:

Allan Nunn May, I have listened with some slight surprise to some of the things which your learned Counsel has said he is entitled to put before me: the picture of you as a man of honour who had done only what you believed to be right. I do not take that view of you at all. How any man in your position could have had the crass conceit, let alone the wickedness, to arrogate to himself the decision of a matter of this sort, when you yourself had given your written undertaking not to do it and knew it was one of the country's most precious secrets, when you yourself had drawn and were drawing pay for years to keep your own bargain with your country—that you could have done this is a dreadful thing. I think you acted not as an honourable but as a dishonourable man. I think you acted with degradation. Whether money was the object of what you did, in fact you did get money for what you did. It is a very bad case indeed. The sentence upon you is one of ten years' penal servitude.

Having uttered nothing in his own defence, still refusing to identify his contacts or help the authorities in any way, May vanished from the public scene to Wakefield Prison, in Yorkshire. His case was like a rehearsal in an empty theatre, a prologue delivered to an unresponsive house before the atmosphere had been created and before the real action of the tragedy had begun. There were still, however, one or two echoes from the case which sound oddly now, in the 1960's, when so much has happened, and when our feelings about this sort of treason have become so firmly fixed.

A month or two after the trial the Association of Scientific Workers in Britain issued a statement calling for a reduction of the "extremely harsh" sentence of ten years passed on May.

It is noteworthy [the statement read] that the maximum sentence under the proposed Atomic Energy Bill is penal servitude for a period of five years. It is clear that no account was taken of Dr. May's positive contribution to the winning of the war by his scientific work, and that the sentence is out of all proportion to the magnitude of the offense committed.

A few days later an independent member of the House of Commons, Mr. W. J. Brown, asked the Home Secretary, Mr. Chuter Ede, if he would review the sentence.

Mr. Brown said that it was perfectly obvious that May was no common criminal—and no traitor in the ordinary sense of the word. He had suffered a much heavier sentence than had been passed on many people who had sold their country for money. The whole issue of atomic bomb secrecy constituted an extremely doubtful ethical area, and would the Home Secretary have another look at the case?

Mr. Ede replied:

It was open to this man to appeal against the sentence, although he would have run certain risks had he done so. It is still open to him to apply for an extension of time within which to lodge an appeal. I do not accept the implications or the statement made by the honourable member. I can understand although I cannot condone the attitude of a man who said he was willing to make knowledge he had acquired generally available. But this man did sell knowledge he had acquired in the service of this country to a foreign power for their private and particular use.

There were, at this, loud cheers in the House.

Just one more attempt was made by the Association of Scientific Workers, when they waited in a deputation upon Mr. Ede in the following year, 1947, and again asked him to reduce the sentence. The deputation was led by the late Professor Harold Laski, and the answer was no.

Part Two • KLAUS FUCHS

Four

•

WHEN THE NEWS OF ALLAN NUNN MAY'S ARREST REACHED THE
atomic research station at Los Alamos, New Mexico, in March
1946, there was not unnaturally some little excitement among the
British scientists and their families there. Here was one of their
own people and he had turned out to be a spy.

One of the wives heard the news first on the radio, and she
came running to tell Klaus Fuchs and others who had been
working there on the atomic bomb for the past year or more.
At once they began asking each other: "Who knew Nunn May?
What was he like?"

"I knew him fairly well," one of the women said. "But I don't
know how you would describe him. He was like—why, he was
rather like Klaus here."

Doctor Fuchs smiled politely, but made no comment. However, he did discuss May's treason, and he doubted whether May
could have told the Russians very much. He had no very high
opinion of Allan Nunn May, either as a scientist or a man.

Even in 1946, before anyone knew about Fuchs' real character, it was perhaps stretching the facts a little far to suggest
there was any real resemblance between the two men. There
were certain superficial similarities, both physical and mental.
They were very nearly of the same age—Fuchs was just eight

months younger. Both were rather detached and noncommittal in their manner. They were serious and shy and self-effacing. Both of them were adorned with the same bulging forehead, the receding hair, the horn-rimmed glasses, the set mouth, and the slightly weak chin. And in their secret hearts, as we now know, both of them thought they had a mission to reform the world. So the pattern was the same. But in the quality of that pattern, its design and emphasis, they were as different as hydrogen and lead. Everything about Fuchs was lighter and more finely made. May was a square man, and Fuchs was lean. Fuchs had a sensitive and enquiring face, a mildly lost air, and this made a great appeal, especially to women. He was just as silent as May, but his silences were endurable. He was woefully short-sighted, but behind the thick lenses his eyes had a certain inward quality that comes usually from reflection, over long periods and alone. His thin body was a good deal stronger and more resilient than it looked. He never played games (because he believed he could never play them well), but he was an exceptionally good dancer, a mountaineer of more than average tenacity, and a skier. The idea of poise, of holding yourself perfectly under control in difficult circumstances, played a very large part in Klaus Fuchs' scheme of life.

From America he came on to Harwell in England after the war, with a great reputation for his work at Los Alamos and New York. He was a senior man at Harwell, the head of one of the most important departments. He did not, of course, rank with Niels Bohr, Einstein, or the other half-dozen at the top. Still, he was well up in the second flight, a distinguished and respected scientist of international standing. By 1949 he was earning a salary of £1800 a year; though a bachelor, he enjoyed the obscure privilege of having a "prefab" house of his own, and he was rated as a possible No. 3 in the Harwell hierarchy, under the director, Sir John Cockcroft, and Professor H. W. B. Skinner.

He had very few close friends, and outside these he was not notably well liked at Harwell by his department or his acquaintances. He was too difficult to know. Despite all his long years in England, he seemed to have had no success in adopting British manners or a British cast of thinking; he remained German, and there were times when his subordinates felt this keenly. But Harwell is a small community, brought together by the brains and not by the social graces of its inmates, and their lives are compulsorily thrown together. By 1949 Doctor Fuchs was established at Harwell in the same way as an officer is established on a ship, a master in a school, or a resident doctor in a hospital. He was known, and he was a fixture. His whole life was there in Harwell for anyone to see. He was a strange man in many things, but there were other strange men in Harwell, too, and his strangeness, his eccentricities, became the accepted and familiar pattern by which he was known.

When he sat down, for example, he had a nervous trick of crossing his knees and constantly turning one of his feet round and round. He was a chain-smoker of cigarettes. And he was a fabulous drinker. He drank, not persistently, not like a soak, but on certain occasions, and with a sort of undergraduate bravado. He drank neat tumblers of gin. He consumed neat whisky by the bottle. And the whole point of this operation was to demonstrate that he remained unmoved, he never turned a hair. At one party he took a Gargantuan draught of spirits, and led the guests on a conga round the house. But this was just lightheartedness. When it was over he summoned up his decorum again; and there he was, Doctor Fuchs, head of the department of theoretical physics, poised and in command, equally ready to drive the guests home or launch into a discussion of isotopes. There were great stories of his drinking prowess. At a celebration in Los Alamos it was Doctor Fuchs who, having filled his own glass all evening, finally put the barman to bed. He was not a drunkard, nobody suggested that. But he was a mighty drinker when he chose.

The one thing that sent him into rages was inefficiency. There was, for the Doctor, a right way of doing things, and to ignore it was nothing less than sheer idleness and silliness. This rule applied to physics, love affairs, domestic life, and, in the end, to politics. In his exasperation at some muddle he would exclaim, "I'll handle it"—and he usually did, extremely well. If a group of people had to be driven to the railway station, or some appointment, he did not much enjoy the spectacle of them standing about politely, and democratically sorting themselves out, deciding which car should be taken, and how they should sit. That was unnecessary and inefficient. Fuchs would advance firmly to his own car. "Come on. Everybody get in. I'll drive you."

Fuchs was an erratic car driver. He adored speed, or rather the risks attendant on speed, not the speed itself. One of his friends recalls driving home with him one night through a drenching storm when the car skidded badly. Fuchs pulled it back onto the right side of the road again. "I love skids," he said. "They give you the opportunity of controlling them."

He had no hobbies and took no regular exercise. There were times when he played chess, and, very occasionally, cards. When his house came to be packed up after his arrest, it was found that besides the standard works on physics, he had a wide and haphazard collection of books, ranging from *Alice in Wonderland,* La Fontaine's *Fables,* Wells' *Outline of History,* to popular novels, religious tracts, and Kravchenko's *I Chose Freedom.* (One year he gave *I Chose Freedom* to several people as a Christmas present.) But he was not a reader outside his own studies; most of these books had been given him by friends. He himself wrote innumerable reports, but never a book.

Once he bought a violin, and taught himself to play. But in recent years he put it away, and few of his friends knew that he possessed it. Apart from this slight interest in music, he cared nothing at all for the arts. He was the great unimpressionable. On sight-seeing tours his friends would implore him, "But you must look at it, Klaus. It's one of the most beautiful pictures [or sculptures, or buildings] in the world, and you will probably never have a chance of seeing it again." He remained unmoved, not lumpish or cynical, but detached and unimpressed.

He would go to the movies as everybody else did at Harwell, but it was impossible to obtain any real reaction from him after the show. He had liked it. He liked them all.

In the society of women he relaxed. He was the kind of man who needs women and that need naturally evoked a response; from his student days onward there was always some woman with whom he was intimate, with whom he would be at ease and talk as he seldom did in the company of men. He was not gay, but he was devoted. And on the woman's side, there was usually a motherly desire to comfort this sincere and introspective man, to draw him out, to nurture him, and give him a haven from his endless searching.

He was not an untidy man, either in his clothes or in the way he ran his house, but there were days when he did not shave and his dark blue beard sprouted in an ugly mat through his pale skin. But in all else he was a precise man. He was the sort of man who can look through a railway timetable in a moment and make clear and exact arrangements for a rendezvous, and he was never late. He was the chairman of a civil servants' committee at Harwell—a committee which settled the domestic affairs of the community, dealing with complaints and deciding who should approach the authorities over the drainage and the water rates and so on—and he was a balanced and excellent chairman.

He was almost a fanatic about security. He was the one who, at declassification conferences, was often opposed to the release of information to the public. He was forever going to the security officer to give him his keys for safekeeping, and he was meticulous in locking up his documents and guarding his speech among nonofficial people. No one ever accused Klaus Fuchs of careless talk; his was the type of bureaucratic mind which is always on the safe side, which keeps secrets when it is quite unnecessary, purely out of ingrained habit and an absurd feeling for the mystique of the official word. As far as possible, he liked affairs to be either black or white; and a genial compromise was, to him, always a mistake. He never mastered the art of talking easily to strangers. He had a sense of humour, but he lacked warmth. He ate sparingly, often without appetite, and he was extravagant in nothing except those endless cigarettes and the occasional showy bouts of drinking.

One of the staff at Harwell with a taste for clerihews—Professor Skinner—wrote this:

"Fuchs
Looks
An ascetic
Theoretic."

There used to be a game in England—the sort of game that is played at a Christmas party in which someone thinks of the name of a man and the rest of the party has to identify him by asking, "What sort of music does he resemble? If he were architecture what period would he be? What painting does he remind you of?" and so on.

In his own mind, perhaps, Fuchs thought of himself as Sydney Smith thought of heaven—"Eating *pâté de foie gras* to the sound of trumpets." But to his friends he was Gothic, his music was Handel, and in painting he reminded them of the mystical, bright colours of El Greco.

He was not a mean man. He paid his father's expenses on a trip to America, and, at the time of his arrest, he was arranging for his dead sister's child to be brought from Germany to school in England. He took great trouble to find a suitable school; he arranged for the boy to live in his own house at Harwell, and he was to pay all the expenses.

In the late 1940's a spot developed on his lung, and he handled this illness in a curious way. There were times when he looked haggard and ghastly white, but he persisted in going on with his work and he never complained. No one then could induce him to see a doctor and go to bed. One of his friends recalls a drive along the Riviera during their summer holidays. The heat was excessive, and the twisting Corniche road near Genoa was full of traffic. Fuchs drove all day with a morose and frantic determination, and he looked as though he would faint at any moment. In the morning, when he was obviously better, he said to his friends: "I took my temperature last night. It was 104."

Then, on other occasions, he would give way—and more than give way—to his illness. He would lie for hours, even days, on end with his face turned to the wall, eating next to nothing, saying nothing, reading nothing, abandoning himself to a trance of physical grief. Nothing could be done with him. He lay there, hour after hour, without speaking or making any sign. Sometimes these morbid fits went far beyond anything created by his illness, for that was adequately looked after by a doctor and he has been cured. Once one of his women friends went to him, and said: "Look, Klaus, why don't you get up? There is no need for you to stay in bed. You are not really ill any longer."

He turned round and answered in a normal voice, "All right. I'll get up if you think so." Then he calmly dressed himself and went out to his office to work.

This queerness was by no means a regular thing with him— it is remembered because it was exceptional. But those friends who had known him best over a long period noted something else which they regard as much more interesting. This was the great change that came over Fuchs at Harwell. In his early student days in the English universities he had been oblivious of what was going on around him, of the little, ordinary things of life. He was not gauche or unwilling, but it would simply never occur to him that he might open a door for a woman or give a present on a birthday or make a gesture of any kind. If he got a new necktie, it was because some woman, unable to bear the ragged knot round his neck any longer, had bought him one. He was a perfect specimen of an abstracted professor in the making. He worked. He worked at home and in the laboratory as though driven by demons. It was the work that mattered. All the rest was a killing of time.

One of Fuchs' colleagues during the war has described his first impression of him. "I thought him," he said, "a colourless, disembodied, and methodical brain."

Now at Harwell in the late 1940's he still worked with the same utter concentration, but in his relationship to the people around him he had developed into a paragon of thoughtfulness and kindness. He was the one who quietly went out to the kitchen and did the washing up after dinner. He remembered on his trips to London to buy cream puffs for a friend who had a passion for them. He would go out at any time of night to meet someone at the station, to run an errand, or sit with a sick friend.

Consequently there were people at Harwell who grew to like Fuchs very much indeed. He was their trusted friend, and he was much more to them than a brilliant, disembodied mind. He had come to England sixteen years before, penniless, unable to speak the language, a refugee from the Nazis in Germany. In those sixteen years he had never been involved in a scandal, had never come to the notice of the police in any way except in so far as he was an alien when war broke out. And now, entirely through his own devoted work with the British and for the British, he had risen to the top in the most elect and difficult of all sciences, the theory of nuclear physics, and they were proud of him in a way.

He was one of the first to arrive at Harwell in 1946, when it was nothing much more than a bleak encampment on a deserted airfield. He had seen it grow up from next to nothing, and he had helped in all the planning. If there was one thing about Fuchs that was entirely apparent, it was his devotion to Harwell. It was his home and the centre of his work, and he loved the place.

His friends knew this. They knew him very well. They knew his house, his habits, his work, his oddities, his income, and his fixed loyalty to his colleagues. And they had known these things over a long period of time.

What they did not know, what they did not conceive by the barest glimmer of an inkling, was that all this was a façade and a lie. It was a lie when they first met him and it had developed now into a lie of such stupendous size that very few of us were going to recover entirely from its consequences. It was not only the fact that he had passed information to the Russians about the atomic bomb—others had done that too, and the Russians could never have made a bomb at that time out of Fuchs' information alone. Nor was it merely the fact that, in a peculiarly horrible and deceitful way, he was a reincarnation of Chaucer's Smiler with the Knife and that he had evoked in his colleagues' minds a deep distrust of one another, for who could be above suspicion after this?

The real issue went much further. We were confronted in Fuchs by a man who carried Allan Nunn May's floundering ethics to their logical and suicidal conclusion. He was Nunn May magnified a hundred times, for where Nunn May was ready to help the Russians against his own people but stopped short at that, Fuchs was prepared to betray all people anywhere at any time. Only his own conscience was to be his guide. According to the dictates of his conscience he was entitled—more than that, he was positively obliged—to turn and turn again. The rules of society, built up through a long and painful history, meant nothing. The undermining of trust, and physical suffering, meant nothing. Only the conscience counted. That was the one thing, in Fuchs' code, that could not be betrayed, and he saw himself as a martyr to it. How that conscience was formed, who gave it the authority—this he did not discuss. The conscience was divine, unquestioned, and inexplicable; it simply gave forth its inevitable light, and one obeyed. There have been anarchists before in the world, but Fuchs was a peculiar kind of anarchist, for he loved not chaos but order. He liked skidding on a wet road, not because of the skidding itself, but because it enabled him to put the car to rights again.

It is probably true that all men love power, even though they hate responsibility, and they will use power whenever they can get it. Fuchs found himself in possession of great power, and he at once went trotting to his divine conscience for instructions as to what he should do with it. He did not pause to ask society for its advice. His conscience was above society. This is the peculiar menace of Fuchs, for if he were to propagate himself, if thousands and tens of thousands of Fuchses and their consciences were let loose on the world, they would be almost as deadly as the worst atomic bomb invented yet.

Split atoms follow at least predictable courses, and the Fuchses do not. It is useful, then, to turn back through Fuchs' life, and see if we can discover where his conscience came from, who made it, and who twisted it to these perverse and unpredictable ends.

Five

•

ONE OF THE THINGS THAT MUST BE PUT DOWN AGAINST THE NAZIS
is that they probably did more toward the corruption of Klaus
Fuchs' mind than anything the Communists ever achieved. They
ruined the Fuchs family just as effectively as some contagious
plague might have done. After the mother had committed suicide,
they put the father in prison. They drove the eldest son and the
younger daughter into exile, and they caused another daughter
to throw herself out of an underground train in Berlin. Finally,
having set their Brown Shirts on to Klaus, the youngest boy, they
forced him too into hiding and converted him into a bitter and
hardened Communist.

The Fuchses were not Jews, and in the beginning they were
not Communist, so they were not natural targets of the Nazis.
They were a Protestant family and they lived in rather poor but
respectable circumstances in the industrial west of Germany.
Doctor Emil Fuchs, the father, was a Lutheran pastor of immense religious faith, and he brought up his family in the belief
that they must always do what they felt to be right whatever
the consequences might be. It was not sufficient merely to know
what was right; you had to act upon it. This was the centre of
his creed: a positive and active Christianity, supported by the
love of God and a firm belief that every man knew within him-

self what was right and what was wrong. It carried him superbly through afflictions which are still unheard of among most families in England and America. He became a Quaker, an active pacifist, and as a member of a group known as the Religious Socialists, he was the first Lutheran pastor to join the Social Democratic Party after World War I.

Doctor Fuchs enjoyed forty years of life in a fairly normal and settled community in Germany before the 1914 war broke out, and in that time his faith became strong. What he could not foresee was the effect of his teachings on children who never knew his stability in their daily lives, who were born and brought up in wars and their aftermath, when all the old values and loyalties were breaking up around them. Life for them became a frantic struggle for existence, before they had fairly got their roots into the ground. The love of God was not as apparent to them as it was to Doctor Fuchs, and consequently there was a great danger in his teaching, for there was always the possibility that his children would absorb one part of it and forget the rest: that they would lose their faith in God, and yet still believe in their absolute right and their duty to take decisions into their own hands, to act as they themselves thought best. This was a dangerous proposition, a demand for positive individual action which was not based on faith but on personal judgment, and it is precisely what destroyed the youngest son.

Klaus was born in the village of Russelsheim, not far from Darmstadt and Frankfurt-am-Main, on December 29, 1911, and christened Emil Julius Klaus. His first memories were of life in provincial towns in the industrial belt where his father travelled from one poor parish to another. He seems to have been happy enough as a small child, but later on he particularly remembered his first act of public defiance soon after World War I was over. This happened one day when there was a celebration for the Weimar Republic, which had succeeded the Kaiser's government.

Not all Germans by any means were ready to accept their defeat and the tame compromise of a Socialist republic. They were willing to erect the Weimar flags on the public buildings, but in privacy they had other views. The flags went up on Klaus' school building, but once the pupils got inside, many of them took off their republican badges and put up the imperial colours instead. At home, no doubt, Klaus had heard a great deal about his father's fervent hopes for the new constitution. So he stuck to his Weimar colours, and the other pupils tore them off him. That was his first ostracism, his first effort at doing what he thought right no matter what the consequences might be. It seems possible that there could have been other incidents as well, for his father's pacifism could hardly have been popular in that atmosphere, and it was still something of a scandal for a pastor to have openly joined a political party.

In 1925, when Klaus was thirteen, his father joined the Society of Friends, and the background of these schooldays is that of a poor, pious, and strictly Quaker home.

Klaus then moved on to the University at Leipzig and was gathered at once into those tortuous and futile undergraduate intrigues which bedeviled university life all over Germany at that time and never ceased or made sense until he left the country for good in 1933. Even in the French and Italian universities in the 1920's there was no real parallel for these political upheavals among the German students, and certainly nothing approaching their violence occurred in England or America. Probably there was nobody in Europe less qualified than the German undergraduates to lay down political rules for themselves or anybody else, and in the absence of any real knowledge of government their half-digested philosophy flew into direct action. They operated in a political vacuum where nothing was established—neither the new Russian Communism nor the new democracy nor the old monarchical ideas of the West, and as yet nobody had foreseen that all these politics were going to be demolished by something quite new and horrible in the world, the doctrine of Fascism. But for the time being this was a grand field of operations for a boy like Klaus Fuchs, with his natural missionary desire to convert and to restore order out of chaos, and he plunged into the struggle with enthusiasm.

First, like his father, he joined the Social Democrats. As a pacifist he did not approve of the party's plans for the rebuilding of the Panzerkreuzer, but he much preferred the Social Democrats to the Communists, who did not even bother to think for themselves—they simply took the party line. To an individualist like Fuchs this was quite impossible. He and he alone was responsible for his decisions and his actions.

Next, according to his own view of his father's teaching, he had to act, and so he joined the Reichsbanner as well. This was already a contradiction of his pacifism, for the Reichsbanner was a semimilitary organisation designed to defend the democrats in case of violence. It was his first break with his father's philosophy, the first stage of the long downhill ride that was going to take him either into Communism or Fascism.

In 1931, when Fuchs was 19, his father was given a professorship of religious science at the Teachers' Training College at Kiel, and the whole family moved to the north. Prior to this they had been living at Eisenach, the industrial town in the Thuringian forest, and now their circumstances were somewhat improved. Fuchs continued studying for his degree in physics and mathematics, and at once picked up the political lines he had left behind at Leipzig. Kiel was a good deal smaller than Leipzig, but he was now an old hand at undergraduate politics, and he began to strike out for himself. He made his first decisive move to the left when he joined a new organisation composed partly of Social Democrats and partly of Communists, and he became chairman of it. This was an unwholesome group on any count. In the first place, no genuine Social Democrat could have

joined it, for it was the persistent policy of the Communist Party
to attack the Social Democrats. The Communists loudly proclaimed the united front of the left against the Nazis and the
right wing, but this did not prevent them from decrying the Social
Democrats as too spineless and inactive, nor from trying to undermine them in every way. As in every other country, the long-
range object of the Communists was, of course, to destroy the
liberals as well as the right wing, but that was something which
Klaus Fuchs and his friends would not see clearly for many years
to come.

There was one other reason why the new Social Democrat-
Communist group was unwholesome, and that was because it
had a secret and treacherous object. It sought to infiltrate the
Nazi Party, to gain the confidence of Nazi members by drawing
them into illegal adventures, and then doublecross them by ex-
posing them at the last minute. As chairman of the group, Fuchs
soon found an admirable occasion for a manoeuvre of this kind.
The Nazis were agitating for a reduction of the university fees.
Very well, Fuchs proposed to them, let us jointly organise a
strike of the students. The Nazis were a little taken aback at this,
but they were ready to discuss the matter. Fuchs waited until
the negotiations were well advanced, and then, without warning
the Nazis, he issued a public pamphlet making it clear just what
had been going on. As a method of making enemies, it would be
hard to find an improvement on this, and indeed the Nazis did
not forget.

Long after, Fuchs said he had some repinings. It had not been
necessary to issue that pamphlet, he reflected. He had violated
some standard of decent behaviour by doing it, and for a long
time he could not straighten out the incident in his mind to
his own satisfaction. Finally he accomplished this by saying
that in a struggle of this kind any such regrets were simply weakness.

Meanwhile he was rapidly moving further to the left. He was

already regarded as unreliable by the Social Democrats for his friendship with the Communists over the pamphlet affair, and then the series of Reichstag elections, beginning in June 1932, gave him the opportunity of going the whole way. Hindenburg had been proposed by the right for Reich President, and the Social Democrats decided not to oppose him with a candidate of their own, lest they should split the vote and let Hitler in. If Hitler were elected he would control the police organisation, and that would be the end of the Social Democrats in Prussia. Fuchs' argument was that you could not stop Hitler by combining with the right. The only way to do it was through a united working-class party, and on this he finally broke with the Social Democrats. He offered himself as a speaker for the Communists at the election, and the Social Democrats expelled him.

When Hindenburg was elected, and von Papen as Reichschancellor dismissed the democratic Prussian government, it was all too painfully clear to Fuchs that he had been right. The Social Democrats were moribund and finished. They did not even have the strength to fight for the dying Prussian government—all they did was to refer the matter to the Reich Central Court. The only place for him now was with the full-blooded, fighting Communists.

It did not occur to him that he and the Communists had played their part in destroying the Social Democrats and the last remaining hope of liberal democracy in Germany. Nor does he seem to have realised that by this time the Communist Party was committed to the deliberate policy of letting Hitler take power so that he could hang himself in the process, and in the resulting chaos the Communists themselves hoped to sweep in and demolish all other parties—right, left, and centre. They turned out to be wrong about that, of course, but, wrong or right, Fuchs appears to have known nothing of it.

He had now performed the full cycle. From a practical democrat of Christian principles and a firm belief in the freedom of the individual, he had developed into a militant Communist, an atheist who had handed over his free will to the Party, and he convinced himself that it had all happened logically, step by step, the whole way.

Now he had touched what he believed to be a firm political bottom. He joined the Communists outright, and he was in his first glow of enthusiasm for the one true party. It was a feeling that called for some act of heroism, and presently he found occasion for that too.

On January 30, 1933, Hitler became Reichschancellor, and soon afterward the Nazis in Kiel felt strong enough to go ahead with their students' strike at the University. The Brown Shirts were called in from the town to parade before the classrooms, and Fuchs, who had something of his father's courage, deliberately showed himself among them. They caught him one day and might have killed him—which would have been no rare thing among all the monstrosities that were sweeping Germany that year. However, in the end, they merely manhandled him and threw him in the river.

If there was one thing needed to confirm Fuchs in his Communism it was that. Now he had suffered for the cause. From now on he was prepared to accept the Party line, whatever it might be—the situation was too critical to permit oneself the luxury of any qualms or doubts.

All that followed helped to confirm the ideas I had formed [he said later]. Not a single party voted against the extraordinary powers which were given to Hitler by the new Reichstag, and in the universities there was hardly anybody who stood up for those who were dismissed either on political or racial grounds; and again you found that people whom you normally would have respected because of their decency had no force in themselves to stand up for their own ideals or moral standards.

In other words, the time of half measures had gone. The fight was on. You either stood up to the Nazis or you were destroyed, and all causes now had become either black or white. There were no halftones in between; you had to be either a Nazi or a Communist.

Very early on the morning of February 28, 1933, Fuchs got up and took a train for Berlin. He had been chosen to attend a Communist students' congress in the capital, and he did not know then that the Nazis would come looking for him that day in Kiel. But he realised it as soon as he bought a newspaper and saw that the Reichstag in Berlin had been burned down the night before. The debacle had begun.

I remember clearly [he said later], when I opened the newspaper in the train I immediately realised the significance [of the Reichstag fire], and I knew that the underground struggle had started. I took the badge of the hammer and sickle from my lapel which I had carried until that time.

And on arrival in Berlin he went into hiding.

There are not now many people in Berlin who survived unscathed the terror that broke out that summer and ultimately spread over the whole world. Hundreds of thousands of Germans were killed, arrested, put into concentration camps, or fled across the borders. In Kiel the Fuchs family was caught along with many others. Klaus' mother had committed suicide the previous year, but the old man was still there, and trenchantly holding to his Socialist views. They put him in prison for several months before he was brought before a People's Court. He stood up, unrepentant, before the judges, declaring that nothing would make him alter his views or prevent him from speaking openly about what he believed to be right. In these early days the Nazis were not yet prepared to obliterate a well-known minister, and there was still a certain respect for the Quakers. There had been an outcry at Doctor Fuchs' imprisonment, and one of the influential Quakers from England was in court. Doctor Fuchs was released, and the Gestapo contented themselves by keeping an eye on him from then on. At the same time they noted in their books at Kiel that Klaus Fuchs, the Doctor's youngest son, was a Communist Party member, that he had escaped arrest, and that his present whereabouts was unknown.

The other three children—Gerhardt, the eldest brother, and the two girls, Kristel and Elisabeth—had by this time also gone over to Communism. Gerhardt managed to avoid arrest, and for a time he and his father ran a car-hire business for getting anti-Nazi refugees out of the country. Eventually Gerhardt escaped to Switzerland, where he obtained treatment for his tubercular infection. Kristel managed to get to America later, and settled down with her husband at Cambridge, Massachusetts. Elisabeth had the most tragic fate of all. She was an artist and she married a Communist sympathiser named Kittowski. They had one child, a son. The family was arrested and put into prison. From prison Elisabeth managed to help in organising her husband's escape to Czechoslovakia. For months she heard nothing from him, but she and the baby were released from prison, and eventually she got word through underground channels that he was in Prague. The strain of this separation, and the danger in which they were all living, began to unhinge Elisabeth's mind. When the Munich treaty was signed, and in March 1939 the Nazis marched into Prague, she became frantic with grief and worry. Her father was travelling with her one day in the Berlin underground. He held her hand, knowing that she might do something desperate, since she was convinced that her husband had been caught in Prague and tortured by the Nazis. He let go her hand for a moment while he took the train tickets out of his pocket, and in that instant she threw herself out on the track and was killed.*

The fate of Klaus had been a good deal easier. The Gestapo

* Kittowski in fact was never caught by the Germans and is still alive.

never found him in Berlin when he arrived there in February 1933. He attended the students' conference which was held surrepetitiously, and received much praise for his work at Kiel. He was advised then by the Party to make his way out of the country so that he could complete his studies abroad and then return one day and help in the building of the new Germany when Hitler's regime had collapsed. As a first step he was asked to attend a United Front rally which was being organised by Henri Barbusse in Paris in August.

After he had been five months in hiding, Fuchs clandestinely crossed the frontier into France in July and made his way to Paris. He was now 21. He had no funds, no friends outside acquaintances in the French Communist Party, and he spoke nothing but German. It happened that about this time a friend of his, a German girl who was engaged to one of his cousins, was living with an English Quaker family in Somerset, England. Fuchs wrote to her from Paris, where he was by now destitute. When the Quaker family heard the story, they sent a generous invitation to Fuchs to come and join them in England so that he could complete his studies. He arrived in England, white-faced, half-starved, with a bundle of dirty linen in a canvas bag, on September 24, 1933.

He told the immigration officer that he had come to England to study physics at the Bristol University, and he gave as a reference the name of the Quaker family in Somerset, saying that they were friends of his father. He was registered on the official records of the Aliens Branch of the Home Office as a refugee; a steady stream of refugees was arriving at this time, and he was given leave to land. Fuchs said nothing about his Communist connections to the immigration officer. He went at once to his Quaker friends in Somerset and remained with them for the next two years.

Already, in 1933, when he was still only 21, Klaus Fuchs was an interesting study in loyalties—especially for those who had been brought up in secure homes in the Western democracies, and who had no real conception of what had been going on in Germany. Already he had betrayed—perhaps that is too strong a word for it, he had abandoned—not one, but several causes. He had walked out on the Social Democratic Party. He had turned his back on both his pacifism and his Christianity. And now he was about to adopt an entirely new nationality. It would have been difficult for anyone to have said precisely where his loyalties lay and where they were going to remain. He had been submitted to frightening experiences—his father says he had been sentenced by the Nazis to be lynched—and they had very nearly finished him.

For his father, who had remained in Germany, and who shortly would be left there alone to bring up the four-year-old child of his dead daughter Elisabeth, the issues were not the same, for Doctor Fuchs had his faith in God, and that was absolute.

The spring and summer of 1933 [Doctor Fuchs wrote] were good to look upon. But my children were scattered, my life's work broken. My friends were in danger; some had fled; others had been imprisoned; many had been killed. And around me was the success of what I knew was the power of destruction and injustice. I hated the beauty of that spring, and I fled the sight of families and the sounds of music. Hiding its terrors behind sparkling life made fate seem doubly cruel. But then came the experience of Christ's presence, and it became stronger and stronger in my being.

Klaus Fuchs had none of this faith to bear him up. He was hungry, threadbare, and bitter. It was probably out of nothing more or less than a natural instinct for self-preservation that he turned toward the only two things that had any appearance of solidity in his life. One was his study of physics, and the other was Communism.

Six

•

FROM THE MOMENT THEY SEIZED POWER THE NAZIS NEVER LOST
sight of the refugees whom they had driven abroad. From 1933 on
they were constantly denouncing these people to the governments
of the countries in which they had settled, and in some cases they
attempted to lure or coerce them back to Germany again. The
Communist Party was equally busy among the refugees, and
rather more successful, for the refugees were an admirable
reservoir from which to recruit new members for the Party. German Communism gave them a link with their homes, and there
was always the prospect that, through Communism, they would
return to Germany once Hitler was ousted. In England, France,
and all the Western democracies new cells of refugee Communists were set up. They profited by the current left-wing
liberalism and anti-Fascism of the West, especially on the outbreak of the Spanish Civil War. They became active in all refugee
organisations, in charitable and religious groups, in working-class
movements, and in the universities. Such societies as these were
obvious points of gravitation for every homeless refugee as soon
as he arrived—there he could find friends, financial help, and
people who could speak his own language—and the Communists
at once set about drawing him into the Party. With the increasing
pressure on the Jews in Germany, and with the fall of Austria

and Czechoslovakia, the flow of these refugees continued steadily, and every refugee was at least a prospective Communist.

The Nazis were very well aware of all this. Their embassies and consulates abroad were supplied by the Gestapo with lists of Germans who had escaped, and they never ceased warning the democracies against these dangerous reds. At times they demanded their extradition.

In November 1934 the German Consul at Bristol reported unofficially to the Chief Constable of the city that Klaus Fuchs was a Communist. This piece of gratuitous information was hardly likely to make any great stir in the Chief Constable's office. In the first place, the German Consul was the representative of the Nazi Government; secondly, he admitted that the source of his information was a Gestapo report from Kiel and it is worth remembering that already in the early 1930's the Gestapo was regarded with a horror which has hardly been eclipsed by the Russian secret police even yet. In any case, it was not illegal in England for a man to be a Communist; indeed, it was a guarantee that he was not a Nazi. Moreover, there were no means of checking Fuchs' past record except from the Germans themselves, and they were scarcely unprejudiced—automatically they branded a man as a Jew or a criminal or a red or all three, if he dared to escape from the fatherland.

This report from the German Consul in Bristol in 1934 was the only definite evidence of Fuchs' Communism that was ever presented, right up to the time of his confession and arrest. It was known, of course, among his friends that he had left-wing views; in Bristol he never made any secret of it. He associated with other German refugees who were known to be strongly anti-Nazi. But he never committed any public act that indicated his allegiance to Communism. He never joined the British Communist Party. He never told the police or any official body, then or later, that he was a Communist. And he never took an active

part in any Communist meeting or demonstration—unless you
count the fact that he was on the committee of a Spanish relief
organisation which was largely concerned with assisting Spanish
refugees.

In forwarding the Gestapo report to the authorities in London,
the Chief Constable commented that Fuchs was not known to
have taken part in any Communist activities in Bristol, nor had
he in any way come to the unfavourable notice of the police.
As an alien, whose permit to stay and work in England had to
be extended from time to time, Fuchs was checked on three separate occasions by the Bristol police—each time with the same
negative result.

It is of course true that, had the police cared to enquire among
Fuchs' friends and neighbours, they would have turned up the
fact that privately he held strong left-wing views—which was
nothing more than they might have suspected already. The
Quaker family with which he stayed used to make Intourist trips
to Russia, and were, at that time, enthusiastic about what they
saw there. But friends and neighbours were hardly likely to
volunteer much information of the boy's political background in
Germany even if they knew anything about it. In any case there
were scores, even hundreds, of Fuchses running round England
in the 1930's; and provided they did not break the peace or
openly make a nuisance of themselves, the police had neither
the means nor the desire to pry into their private lives.

Fuchs, in fact, was living a very quiet life indeed. It was as
though his recent experiences in Germany had exhausted him
and drained him of all desire for action. The record of the next
six years in England is one of uneventful and continuous work
in the universities, while that excellent brain took hold of its
subject to the exclusion of almost everything else.

For the first year he stayed in the country with his Quaker
friends, eating very little, learning English, reading his books,

seeing very few people. He was a shy and unobtrusive visitor in the house. Those who knew him then describe him as an exceptionally gentle young man; he would never have hurt a fly. And he was grateful for what was being done for him. Soon after his arrival he was taken down to the University of Bristol, and there he met Professor Nevill Mott of the Physics Department who spoke fluent German. Mott heard the story of how Fuchs had all but completed his degree in physics in Kiel when he was forced to go into hiding, and it was arranged that he should attend the Bristol University free of charge. In addition to this, Fuchs was helped by the Academic Assistance Council and the Society for the Protection of Science and Learning. In October 1934 (when the German Consul no doubt got to hear about him) he entered the University as Mott's first research student. About the same time his Quaker friends moved into the city, and Fuchs moved with them. Later, when a little money reached him through the charitable institutions, he moved into rooms of his own in the suburb of Redlands.

The physical laboratories of Bristol University have had few students with the ability of Klaus Fuchs. He worked with a persistent, methodical concentration, and there was very little in his life but his work. In 1937 he was awarded his doctorate of philosophy in mathematical physics, and at the same time he was given a research scholarship to continue his studies under Professor Max Born at Edinburgh. It was not a particularly good scholarship, for Fuchs was still an alien and quite unknown. Professor Mott says now that he possibly underrated Fuchs' abilities at the time, but his later success in physics was certainly not apparent then. But he did well at Edinburgh. He began to contribute accounts of his original research to the scientific journals; he wrote a thesis "On Some Problems of Condensation Quantum Dynamics and Stability of Nuclei"; and within two years got his doctorate of science in theoretical physics. In 1939,

on taking this degree, he was awarded a Carnegie Research
Scholarship, and he continued to work at Edinburgh.

Meanwhile, through these years, Fuchs was treating himself
to a thoroughgoing study of the philosophy of Karl Marx in the
privacy of his bedroom at home. He described this later in his
confession:

> The idea which gripped me most was the belief that in the past
> man has been unable to understand his own history and the forces
> which lead to the further development of human society; that now,
> for the first time, man understands the historical forces and he is able
> to control them, and that therefore for the first time he will be really
> free. I carried this idea over into the personal sphere and believed that
> I could understand myself and that I could make myself into what I
> should be.

The method was pythagorean, and the object messianic: the
approach to glory by numbers. In Germany events had happened
so rapidly and so violently; the struggle had been so immediate
and so personal. But here was the philosophy behind it, the
explanation and the justification, the indication of the way ahead.
Das Kapital captivated him, just as it was captivating so many
others in the universities just then. But Fuchs' faith was doubly
strong, for he had already fought for the cause in Germany, and
now, having been brought up in the habit of religion, but having
abandoned Christianity, he was desperately in need of something
to replace it.

All this he wrestled with quite alone. He never tried to convert
anybody else; indeed, in a political conversation he tended to
retreat more and more into the private certainties of his own
mind and keep silent. Equally, there is no ground for believing
that all through these six years he was in England he was acting
as an agent for either the German or the Russian Communists.
To a great extent he lost touch with Germany. He corresponded
innocuously from time to time with his father (who was not a

Communist), but most of his old Communist acquaintances inside Germany were either dead, imprisoned, or in hiding. He himself went abroad only once, on a visit to his brother, who by now had escaped to Switzerland. He saw his sister Kristel once very briefly, when she passed through England on her way from Germany to the United States in 1936. In any case, at the time of Fuchs' escape from Germany in 1933 it was not the established practise of the Russian Intelligence Service to employ non-Party members abroad—this came later. Fuchs, moreover, was still not in possession of secret information; up to 1939 there was a free—even an eager—interchange of information on nuclear physics throughout the world.

As for the effect of England itself and the life of a democracy upon Fuchs, it is impossible to say very much. As the years went by, he did tend to become less political in his conversation and more engrossed in his work. It has been suggested by one of the scientists who knew him well that Communism was for Fuchs a kind of Sunday observance. The faith was always there in the background, but he had only a certain amount of time to give to it. Like a businessman who is involved in his affairs all the week, he kept his religion in a separate compartment of his mind, and for the most part it did not impinge on his work in the laboratory. He never felt strongly enough to enlist in the International Brigade in Spain, and it may have been that by the outbreak of war in 1939 there was a certain weakening of his Communism. Certainly, he confessed later, he received a jolt when Molotov and Ribbentrop signed the Russo-German pact. Up to that time he had automatically accepted the idea that most of the things you heard about Soviet Russia were deliberate lies. But here was a solid, avowed, and indigestible fact: the Russians had gone over to the Nazis, the people he most loathed in all the world. But he explained this away by reassuring himself that Russia had signed the pact simply to gain time so that she could expand her influence against Germany in the Balkans. And then, when finally Hitler *did* attack Russia in 1941, he observed with delight that it was precisely so.

For a time also he found Russia's attack on Finland in 1940 an even more difficult pill to swallow. But this, too, was susceptible to logic, once one worked it out: Russia was simply preparing her defences against *all* imperialistic powers. Had not France and England themselves been thinking in 1940 of invading Finland?

He succeeded, then, in resolving his doubts—but at least he did have doubts, and that was a considerable improvement upon his earlier attitude, when he accepted the Party line without question. He was beginning to think again for himself. His six years in England had gone a long way toward restoring his self-confidence and his sense of security. But the trouble with Fuchs was that he never knew when to stop. His self-confidence developed into arrogance—not an outward arrogance that required public display, but the inward and convinced arrogance of a genuinely introspective mind that never comes out into the open and submits itself to criticism. He fought his campaigns for the health, wealth, and happiness of mankind within the confines of his own skull.

In 1939, however, it was not beyond the bounds of possibility that, given a little more time, in the safe seclusion of Edinburgh, he might have become a little clearer still on the subject of Russian Communism. Certainly he was beginning to accept the English way of life. He was now 27. He spoke English with a German accent, but fluently, and he had made English and Scottish friends. On July 17 he applied for British naturalisation.

On the face of it there was no reason why he should not have been naturalised then. He was supported by the Quakers and the universities. For six years he had been a loyal citizen, and his postgraduate work in the British laboratories had been remarkably good. But by July it was too late. The war began before his application could go forward, and from September 1939 all such naturalisations of enemy aliens were, for the time being, put aside. This was a pity, for, as an enemy alien, he was now submitted to an experience which may well have shaken his faith in democracy, if he ever had any such faith.

On November 2, 1939, when the country had already been at war with Germany for two months, Fuchs was summoned before the Aliens Tribunal at Edinburgh. He had been classified by the Home Office as a refugee from Nazi oppression, and there was now an investigation into his record.

When Fuchs was finally arrested, after the war, it was asserted that he had declared himself to be a Communist before this Tribunal, and consequently the authorities should have been on their guard from that moment forward. But this was not so; Fuchs made no such admission. All the Tribunal had before it was a letter from Professor Max Born of Edinburgh University saying that Fuchs had been a member of the Social Democratic Party in Germany between 1930 and 1932. And, in view of his excellent record in Britain, the Tribunal exempted him from the special restrictions which were then applicable to enemy aliens. He had to report to the police, but that was all. Fuchs went back to his work at the University.

This was the cold-war period, when there was as yet no bombing of civilian towns and no real activity on the Western Front. But with Hitler's attack on France and the Low Countries in the following summer, this picture altered entirely. Britain was now faced with an acute national emergency, and the prospect of invasion. There were obvious reasons for keeping the closest check upon all German nationals. Quite apart from the question of their loyalty—and there was no time to investigate it then— refugees from Germany were likely to be one of the first targets of the Gestapo if Britain were to be invaded. In addition, the food shortage was starting, and no adequate staff or accommodation was available for the internees. There was therefore an urgent need to get them out of the country. Fuchs was interned under the General Order of May 1940.

He was sent first to the Isle of Man in the Irish Sea and then transported across the Atlantic to the Sherbrooke camp near Quebec in Canada. All this was done in some haste and confusion, for the country was absorbed in fighting for its own existence at the time. Without doubt some of the internees were compelled to live under harsh conditions during the early stages of the evacuation. Fuchs was bundled unceremoniously aboard a ship where some of the prisoners felt they were treated more as criminals than ordinary human beings. He at least was luckier than those aboard another internee ship, the *Arandora Star*, which was torpedoed and sunk in 1940 by a German U-boat.

Some of the indignities the enemy aliens suffered seem grotesque now, though perhaps understandable when one remembers the strains and the dangers of the time. The ship in which Fuchs crossed from Liverpool to Quebec was the *Ettrick*, and the journey took a fortnight. A strict discipline was enforced, and in his daily inspection tours around the ship the captain had his presence announced by a hunting horn, so that the prisoners were warned in advance to spring to attention. The papers relating to them had been sunk in the *Arandora Star*, and this meant that on their arrival in Canada nobody for a time knew exactly who they were. There were a group of German clergymen on board, and for some strange reason in Canada it was assumed that they were Nazi parachutists in disguise who had dropped on Rotterdam during the frightful raid which almost destroyed the city; and they were treated as such. They and the others were greeted with jeers of "How's Hitler?" and comments which were a good deal more thoroughgoing than that. Then, on another occasion, a hearty British major assembled the prisoners before him. Most of their families had been murdered, imprisoned, or ruined by Hitler, and many of them had barely escaped the Nazis with their own lives. Consequently they were a good deal astonished when the Major declared: "I'm British and I am loyal to my King. You are Germans, and you think you have got to be loyal to Hitler. As long as that's clear and we understand one another we will get along together all right." On still another occasion, when the prisoners were making a protest —it was a minor matter concerned with their unwillingness to use prisoner-of-war notepaper or something of the kind—the guards turned their rifles on them.

Since men probably resent indignity more than anything else, especially indignity that is founded upon misunderstanding and injustice, it seems possible that Fuchs began to harbour a resentment against the democracies. He would hardly have been human if he had not.

The confusion still persisted in Canada after Fuchs' arrival, for there had been no time to sort out the prisoners properly in England before their embarkation. Fuchs, now wearing a prisoner's uniform with a large, colored patch on the back, was placed in a camp designed to accommodate avowed and unrepentant Nazis. He found one friend there, however, a man named Hans Kahle, who had also been sent to Sherbrooke by mistake. It is a matter for speculation now as to just how much Fuchs may have been affected by his internment and his meeting with this man Kahle.

Fuchs himself had no specific complaint to make later about his internment beyond saying that he realised that, at the time, Britain "could not spare good people to look after the internees" and that being deprived of newspapers he was prevented from knowing how the British were getting on in the war and from learning more about the real character of the British people. Presumably what he meant (but did not care to say) was that

up to 1940 he was not at all sure that the British were seriously
determined to fight the Nazis: that was a job which ultimately
the Russians would have to tackle.

At all events, his internment had cut him off from his work,
and it is not impossible that in the idleness of camp life he
turned to the other and secret passion of his life—the study of
Russian Communism—and refreshed his faith therein. Certainly
Hans Kahle would have assisted him in this matter, for Kahle
was a case-hardened Communist who had been through the
mill from 1935 on—a much older man than Fuchs and highly
persuasive. He was born in Berlin in 1899, and is reported to
have been an officer in the Reichswehr before he became a Communist adventurer. He was in the Soviet Union in 1935 and
1936, and subsequently commanded a unit of the Republican
Army in the Spanish Civil War. In Spain he was regarded as a
representative of the OGPU.

In 1939 Kahle came to England, where he wrote a book on
the civil war, and quickly fell in with well-known British Communists. He was also active in working among organisations
for the relief of refugees from Germany and Spain until war
broke out, when he was interned and sent to Canada.

Later Kahle was released in order to work under Professor
J. B. S. Haldane at the Admiralty in London. Throughout the
rest of the war he was a Communist organiser and propagandist,
and a member of the executive council of the German Communist Party in Britain. Possibly he was then still on the staff
of the OGPU. Soon after the war he went to the Soviet Zone
in Germany, was given an important police post, and died there
in 1947.

This man was the close friend and companion of Fuchs during
the six odd months they were together in Canada, at first in a
camp of pronounced Nazis.

It is not suggested that Hans Kahle drew Fuchs into the

Russian espionage net—Fuchs has said he did not—but it is
possible that he reported to the Russians that Fuchs was a
promising prospect. If he did make such a report, the Russians
did nothing about it. They were not always, as we shall see,
remarkably efficient. Kahle and Fuchs met only once again, when
they had both returned to England, at a Free German Youth
organisation meeting.

Fuchs got no black marks against him in camp. He was a
docile prisoner, and he took only a normal part in the camp
politics. Once he joined a protest against the appointment of the
son of the former German Crown Prince as camp leader. (The
young man had been studying in England when war broke out,
and was regarded as a Nazi sympathiser.) On another occasion
he protested again when there was a report that Jewish internees
were to be exchanged for Canadian prisoners in Germany. But
Fuchs was not notably obstreperous on these issues. There was,
however, one other interesting fact which indicates how devious
are the threads that pass through an espionage pattern, some of
them leading nowhere. While in camp Fuchs used to receive
papers and magazines from Israel Halperin, a professor of mathematics at Queen's University, Kingston, Ontario. Halperin, who
was born of Russian parents in Canada, was closely questioned
by the Canadian Royal Commission in 1946, and finally ac-
quitted. Fuchs says he never met Halperin, and does not know
why Halperin sent him the magazines—except that, just possibly,
Halperin might have got Fuchs' name from his sister Kristel in
Massachusetts. Halperin crops up again in another way in the
Fuchs case; when the Canadian police raided Halperin's home
they found an address book, and in that book was the name of
Fuchs. This information was available to the authorities in 1946
—a good three years before Fuchs was arrested.

But a good deal too much can be made of this. Halperin's
address book contained many names of men who had nothing

whatever to do with espionage. The mere appearance of the name Fuchs in that list in 1946—or of any other name—could not have led to immediate suspicion. It well might have been included simply because Halperin had been asked to send magazines to Fuchs in camp. Still, the connection is there, and it remains one of the bypaths of the story that has not been satisfactorily explained.

Fuchs remained under internment in Canada for the rest of 1940 (consequently missing the worst of the air blitz on England) but his friends were working for him. Professor Born and other scientists who knew and valued his work pressed for his release. And by now the authorities in England had had an opportunity to check on the men who had been so hurriedly sent away in the crisis. In January 1941 Fuchs was released. He returned at once to his research work at Edinburgh University.

Seven

•

IN THE SPRING OF 1941 PROFESSOR RUDOLF PEIERLS OF THE Birmingham University wrote to Fuchs in Edinburgh, asking him if he would be interested in undertaking some work of a special nature at Birmingham. The salary was £275 a year. The job was temporary, but would probably continue for an unforeseeable length of time. If Fuchs liked to come down to Birmingham to discuss the matter his expenses on the journey would be paid.

Professor Peierls was already working secretly on the atomic bomb, and he needed assistants—more particularly an assistant who was competent to make elaborate mathematical calculations. The difficulty was that most of the abler English physicists had by now been pressed into work on radar and other immediately essential wartime research, and good men were hard to find. It was necessary to look among the enemy aliens.

Peierls had known Fuchs only slightly before the war, but he had read some of his research papers, and he knew that Professor Mott of Bristol, Professor Born, and others thought highly of his abilities. On his record he appeared to be precisely the man for the job.

The interview took place in Birmingham and was satisfactory. Fuchs was not told the full nature of the work; he was simply informed that it was urgent, it was secret, and it was connected with the war; and he accepted the job. The problem now for Peierls was to get the appointment approved by the authorities in London.

The security services were consulted, and they put forward the facts. There was the report from the German Consul at Bristol, which had to be regarded as a tainted source. Apart from this, there was nothing against Fuchs; he had studied for seven years in England, he had applied for naturalisation, he had been interned and then released, and now he was engaged on research into theoretical physics at Edinburgh. Apart from the fact that he was an enemy alien at no point in this record had he given grounds for suspicion. However, it was only reasonable for the time being to put Fuchs on a low security rating—he should not be given access to more classified work than was strictly necessary. And it had to be estimated that, if he did give any information, he was more likely to give it to the Russians than the German enemy. That was security's report on Fuchs in 1941.

But in England it is not the business of the security services to say whether or not a man shall be given a job. Their function is advisory—to put forward the known facts and interpret them. It is the responsibility of the Government department concerned to decide whether they shall employ the man. In this case the department concerned was the Ministry of Aircraft Production, for all work on atomic energy had recently been put under its control. The Ministry just then was engaged in producing aircraft to fight the Battle of Britain, and pronounced views were held by Mr. Churchill and his cabinet: anyone, they argued, who was able to help Britain toward the winning of the war ought to be pressed into service, and at once. Fuchs was employed. And since it was manifestly absurd to ask him to engage in the work without telling him what it was about, he was later given access to classified material in Birmingham.

He began work in May 1941 and signed the Official Secrets

Act. Since he was poor and alone, the Peierls family found room
for him in their house in Birmingham, and he continued living
with them, as an intimate member of their household, until
toward the end of his stay in England in 1943, when he moved
to quarters of his own. Through all this time—more than two
years—he never indicated, by anything he said or was observed
to do, that he was in touch with the Russians. The University
staff and his friends were entirely without suspicion. They found
him shy, rather silent, and abstracted. He was quite hopeless at
the business of looking after himself; unless someone in the
Peierls household had sewn on his buttons, helped him buy
his Christmas presents, and occasionally taken him out to social
gatherings, none of these things would have been done. He
returned from his work each evening, and if nobody prevented
him he simply went to his room and continued to work again
halfway through the night. He was not disagreeable to live with.
He liked children, he was fond of dogs, and in a mild, unworldly
fashion he assisted at (in the French sense), rather than took
part in, the family and University gatherings. When he first
arrived in Birmingham his face became paralysed with some
infection, but as a rule he seemed to enjoy at least an anaemic
good health. He had bad teeth and preferred soft foods—
especially eggs and puddings. He made occasional trips up
to London, sometimes in connection with his work, but otherwise
seldom went outside Birmingham.

There was just one incident—it was hardly even an incident
—that might have indicated to the scientists in Birmingham that
they had a strange man amongst them. It was a New Year's
Eve party. They were singing Russian songs and Fuchs was
observed standing a little apart from the others, with a look of
transcendental exaltation on his face—a look of such rapture that
the woman who saw it imagined that he must suddenly have
fallen in love.

Six months after Fuchs arrived in Birmingham the organisation

known as "Tube Alloys" was set up to co-ordinate the work of the
atomic scientists in the various universities. It was not conducted
as an ordinary government ministry, with a hierarchy of civil
servants, but was a small and very secret affair, with unobtrusive
offices in Old Queen Street, Westminster. It had a miniature
staff, headed by Sir Wallace Akers of Imperial Chemical Industries, and Mr. Michael Perrin, also of I.C.I., who was brought
in as his assistant. They were directly responsible to the Lord
President of the Council (Sir John Anderson) and the Prime
Minister. One of their duties was to act as a clearing house for
information as the work on atomic energy progressed. The
scientists engaged on the project in Oxford, Cambridge, Birmingham, and elsewhere were asked to send in monthly reports
which could be disseminated among themselves so that redun-
dancies could be avoided and the work would march forward
evenly. The man who never failed in bringing in his reports
on time—who never pleaded that he was too busy, or that he
was occupied with an experiment that could not wait—was
Klaus Fuchs. And his reports were lucid, well-written, and precise. When asked to interpret them for other scientists who
were not working in the same field, he also had a flair for re-
ducing their technicalities to simple, effective language.

Very soon Professor Peierls in Birmingham was delighted with
the choice he had made of an assistant, and by 1942 he realised
he had acquired something of inestimable value—a perfectly
methodical, calculating brain. More than that, Fuchs had a
talent for understanding any problem put to him, and he learned
with astonishing rapidity. He could be asked to tackle any
calculation and one could rely entirely upon his results.

The work at Birmingham was mainly concerned with the
gaseous diffusion process of separating the uranium isotopes,
which was still in the experimental stage both in Britain and
the United States, and was only one of several possibilities then

being explored. Professor Peierls was a gaseous diffusion enthusiast, and Fuchs, working away in his private world of mathematics, soon became an enthusiast as well.

In 1942 Fuchs again applied for naturalisation as a British
subject, and he had the strong backing of the "Tube Alloys"
directorate. Enemy aliens were naturalised only in exceptional
cases during the war, and the reason given here was that Fuchs
was engaged on work of national importance. He had to become
a British citizen in order to be given access to certain prohibited
places in connection with his work.

There was a police investigation. The eight-year-old report
of the German Consul was again brought up, and it was still
the only evidence against him. Fuchs himself was examined at
an open hearing—the British procedure is very similar to the
system in the United States—and on August 7, 1942, on being
naturalised, he took the following oath of allegiance:

I, Emil Julius Klaus Fuchs, swear by Almighty God that I will be
faithful and bear true allegiance to His Majesty, King George the
Sixth, His Heirs and Successors, according to law.

When he took that oath Fuchs was in active and regular contact with a Russian agent. He established that contact very soon
after he arrived in Birmingham in 1941, and it was not the
Russians who had come to him—he himself had approached
them first and had offered to pass information.

It was not difficult for Fuchs to get in touch with the Russians.
Through the refugee organisations and the universities he knew
a number of Communists who had reached England from Germany since 1933, and it was one of these who passed him on
to Simon Kremer, the secretary to the Soviet Military Attaché in
London.

Throughout his association with Kremer Fuchs knew him
only by the name of "Alexander," and never discovered his real

identity. But Kremer was quite a familiar though a minor figure among diplomats and military people in London during the war. His full name was Simon Davidovich Kremer and he was a Russian, born in Gomel in 1900. He arrived in England to take up his post at the Russian Embassy two years before the war, accompanied by his wife and their two small children. His job was, without doubt, merely a cover for more important activities. He left England toward the end of the war, before the Canadian spy net was discovered, and long before Fuchs' arrest.

What made Fuchs suddenly decide to turn active traitor in 1941? We have his own version of the matter:

Shortly after my release [from internment] I was asked to help Professor Peierls in Birmingham on some war work. I accepted it, and I started work without knowing at first what the work was. I doubt whether it would have made any difference to my subsequent actions if I had known the nature of the work beforehand. When I learned about the purpose of the work I decided to inform Russia, and I established contact through another member of the Communist Party. Since that time I have had continuous contact with persons who were completely unknown to me, except that I knew they would hand over whatever information I gave them to the Russian authorities. At this time I had complete confidence in Russian policy, and I believed that the Western Allies deliberately allowed Russia and Germany to fight each other to the death. I therefore had no hesitation in giving all the information I had, even though occasionally I tried to concentrate mainly on giving information about the results of my own work.

The phrase "another member of the Communist Party" is interesting, for it indicates that, even though he had no contact with the Party in England, he still regarded himself as a member.

Certainly the timing was important. In June 1941, when Fuchs first began to work on the atomic bomb, the Nazis attacked Russia, and then all those anxious doubts about the Russo-German pact and the invasion of Finland were swept out of Fuchs' mind. There followed through the ensuing months Stalin's persistent demand (echoed by the Communist Party all over the world) for a "second front"—an invasion by the Western allies of western Europe so that the strain on Russia would be relieved. When time went on and that demand was not answered, when Moscow nearly fell, when the battle for Stalingrad was fought and the losses of the Russians were frightful, it might indeed have seemed to Klaus Fuchs that his chosen people were being left to bear the brunt. He felt an ardent burning to do something for the cause. There were many other people in England at the time who felt the same way; Mrs. Churchill was organising her Russian Relief Committee, and an intensely pro-Russian feeling spread over Britain. Workers redoubled their labours in the factories, and there was great enthusiasm when the first British arms were sent off to heroic Russia on the Murmansk run. But few people in England had either the means or the necessary arrogance to do what Klaus Fuchs did. He took copies of his monthly reports of his work on atomic energy and gave them to Simon Kremer in London. That was his contribution to the heroes of Stalingrad and to the winning of the war.

He had at least four meetings with Kremer in London between the end of 1941 and the end of 1942. Since it was not always easy for him to get away from Birmingham during the working week—it is a train journey of several hours from Birmingham to London—the meetings were fixed at weekends and in the evening. The first was at a private house to the south of Hyde Park, not far from the Russian Embassy in Kensington Palace Gardens. Here he met just one man, a Russian, who spoke English and called himself "Alexander" and seemed to be familiar with his surroundings. Fuchs, a meticulous man, may have had some doubts as to whether his contact—this man "Alexander"— was genuine, and whether the information was actually getting through to the Russians, because, soon after this first meeting, he went openly to the Russian Embassy to make enquiries, a thing that was absolutely forbidden to agents; and he can hardly have been thanked by the Russians for it. He was reassured, however, for he took up his appointments with Kremer again—usually in quiet residential streets or at crowded bus stops.

There was then, and still is, a technique in spying. It is capable of infinite variation but certain basic rules exist, such as the obvious one that forbids the spy to do anything as foolhardy as paying a visit to a Soviet Consulate or Embassy. Some time before the war the Russian Intelligence Service was reorganised and spies were also forbidden to have any connection with the local Communist Party. These local parties were still used as a recruiting ground for spies but immediately a man was chosen he was obliged to break off all association with known Communists.

Under the new arrangements the Russians found it much more profitable to work through traitors—ideological foreigners like Klaus Fuchs—than through their own nationals, who tended on occasion to be atrociously heavy-handed in the unfamiliar surroundings of the West. The Russians themselves supplied the director of each net; he was usually placed in a country outside the one his net was spying on.

The employment of traitors also called for a new kind of dealing since few of them entered the service for money. Nevertheless, it was necessary to bind them to make sure they would not weaken or turn again, and so the Russian Intelligence Service forced money, however small in amount, on their agents, and obtained receipts—which were useful for blackmailing purposes in case of necessity.

Russian agents are trained in the double life—this was no discovery of Fuchs', as he appears to have imagined—and by the use of cover names and other devices they were all kept in separate compartments. The object here, of course, was to ensure that if a man was discovered he could give only limited information about his actual contacts. The main channels of communication were normally through Russian embassies and legations. They, in turn, used diplomatic couriers, who passed regularly to Moscow. Alternately, coded messages were sent by illegal radio stations.

The meeting places most favoured for spies and couriers were never private houses. Crowded streets and underground stations were found more private since for the most part the contact lasted only a few minutes, just long enough to pass a document in a folded newspaper or a piece of microfilm in a cigarette.

As a rule spies made no signal of recognition when they met, but moved off to another place where the information was handed over, and arrangements were then made for the next meeting. As a precaution a third man, unknown to the other two, sometimes stood by to make sure that the meeting was not observed. There were counter-counterespionage measures as well—coat-trailing operations designed to discover just what security measures were being taken by the country which was being spied on.

All these matters are fairly common knowledge now as a result of the Canadian investigations and the defections of so many Russians and other Communists to the West. But in 1941 and 1942 (when it was hardly to be expected that Russia was already implacably determined to undermine her allies) these things were far from commonplace. Fuchs had to learn the new conspiratorial technique from the beginning and he showed a remarkable aptitude for it: the Russians could have had few agents as precise as he was, few men as exact in their memory, as clear in exposition, as punctual and as eager.

It was in October 1941 that Fuchs began passing information in the form of carbon copies of his reports, which he had typed himself, or manuscript in his own handwriting. All this information came from his own brain and was the result of his own work. If he had other information at the time, he did not give it. It seems possible, then, that in this early stage he may have soothed his conscience by reassuring himself that, after all, this information was his own property. He had produced it; it was his to give away where he wished. But if these reservations did exist in his mind, they did not last.

At the end of 1942 "Alexander" disappeared, and Fuchs was told that from then on he would be dealing with a new contact, a woman. In addition, the rendezvous was changed—no doubt to suit Fuchs' convenience—from London to Banbury. Banbury is a market town some forty miles from Birmingham. The new series of meetings began there in 1942, and continued at intervals of two or three months. On each occasion Fuchs took an afternoon train down from Birmingham during the weekend, and then walked out along a country road just outside the town. The woman waited for him there. She did not live at Banbury; she came there specially for these meetings, then left by train, no doubt for London. Just once they had a rendezvous in a café opposite Snow Hill station in Birmingham.

There have been many assessments of what Fuchs may have given the Russians through 1943. Certainly in the period 1941-1943 he would have been able to tell them that we now considered the uranium bomb was a definite possibility. He could have—and in fact did—give them the results of his own calculations on the theory of the gaseous diffusion process for separating the isotopes of uranium, and the fact that U-235 produced in that way might be used in an atomic bomb.

He could also have furnished his own calculations of the amount of U-235 needed, and of the efficiency of the explosion.

Doctor Karl Cohen, of Columbia University, has commented, in a letter to the Joint Committee on Atomic Energy in Washington, on the state of Fuchs' knowledge at that time. He wrote:

Fuchs' name appeared on theoretical papers on the gaseous diffusion process to my certain knowledge in 1942, and I believe as early as 1941. Because of visits to this country of Peierls and others in early 1942, when the relative merits of the Birmingham and Columbia versions of the diffusion process were discussed at length, . . . it is clear that before Fuchs' arrival he had good knowledge of the American plans for the gaseous diffusion plant. It is important to bear in mind that because of Fuchs' grasp of the theoretical principles involved, which interrelate the process variables so that the choice of a few determines the remainder within narrow limits, he would be able to reconstitute our whole program from only scattered pieces of information. Thus, even before his arrival in New York, when he obtained full and detailed information, he could have transmitted a very good outline of the American gaseous diffusion project.

Doctor Cohen (with some justice) permitted himself to add: "Compared to these consequences, Fuchs' betrayal of the personal integrity of scientists is of minor importance. Nevertheless it was a blow which all scientists bitterly resent." This was a point that had not yet occurred to Fuchs himself in 1943, though it was going to overtake him with some force later on. Meanwhile he continued meeting his woman contact (she has never been arrested), and toward the end of 1943 he told her that he had been selected to go to the United States as a member of the British team which was to continue work on the gas diffusion process in New York.

Precise instructions were then given him by the woman for making contact again with the Russians in New York. He was to go to a street corner on the lower East Side on a Saturday, carrying a tennis ball in his hand. There he would see a man carrying a book with a green binding, and wearing gloves, with an additional pair of gloves in his hand. This man would be known to him as "Raymond" (it was actually Harry Gold, who was arrested in 1950, and who is now serving a sentence of thirty

years in the United States). The two men would then take a
taxi to a restaurant on lower Third Avenue, where Fuchs would
hand over his information and arrangements would be made
for their future meetings.

In November 1943 Professor Peierls, Fuchs, and others embarked at Liverpool on the troopship *Andes* for the United
States.

Wing Commander Henry Arnold (left) and William James Skardon,
security officers at Britain's atomic research station at Harwell

Dr. Nunn May,
leaving London by plane
after his release from prison

Bruno Pontecorvo

Klaus Fuchs
at the time of his arrest

Sir John Cockcroft, director of the Harwell research project

Harry Gold.
David Greenglass is seen behind him.

Lord
Chief Justice
Goddard

Eight

•

EXISTENCE ON £275 A YEAR IN WARTIME ENGLAND WAS HARDLY
luxurious, even for an active bachelor with a double life. Up to
this point Fuchs had been a lean and hungry-looking man. The
gradual change in his outward manner probably dates from this
journey across the Atlantic in the troopship *Andes*. After his two
crossings as an internee the voyage seemed a great luxury to him,
and he was lively and—for him—in high spirits. He was travelling
with friends, and as a representative of the British Government
(for he had been made a temporary civil servant); he was going
to work that he loved, and now, at the approach of his 32nd
birthday, he had an established reputation. In particular, he had
recently been much congratulated upon a paper on the control
of a diffusion cascade which had been of considerable value to
the Americans. His conspiratorial life was untroubled by any
misgivings or hesitations, and his conscience had arrived, no
doubt, at some sort of a mystical peace with itself.

He landed with the Peierls in early December, and they proceeded at once to Washington to sign the usual security undertaking with the United States Government. There was no further
investigation into Fuchs' credentials—he had been cleared by the
British authorities as an accredited member of the British mission—and in the ensuing two-and-a-half years while he was in

the United States no other check was made on him.

From Washington he went to the Taft Hotel in New York. Subsequently he moved to the Barbizon-Plaza and then to an apartment of his own at 128 West 77th Street. He visited his sister Kristel in Cambridge, Massachusetts, within a few days of his arrival—she had now settled permanently with her husband and children in the United States—and he continued to keep in touch with them throughout his stay in the country. There was indeed a plan at one time for the family to come and live with him in New York, but it fell through when, the following year, he was posted to Los Alamos.

Almost from the moment of his arrival in New York Fuchs was exceptionally busy. Starting on December 7, 1943, he attended a series of meetings which enabled the Americans and British teams to clear their ideas about the gas diffusion process with one another, and plan their future operations together. At this time the scientists working on this part of the atomic energy project were divided into two groups: those at Columbia University, who were mainly engaged on research, and those at the Kellex Corporation, where the large-scale gas diffusion plant was designed.

It was soon realised that the best contribution the British could make would be to help on the theory of the control of the gaseous diffusion plant, and Fuchs was specifically asked to make numerical calculations for its design. At the conclusion of the December meetings, part of the British team went home while Peierls, Fuchs, and some others remained to co-operate with the Americans. From this time forward Fuchs was intimately connected with the work, both at Columbia University and at the Kellex Corporation. He had an office at the British centre in Wall Street and he was a frequent visitor to both laboratories. He did little else but work; it filled all his days. One can imagine that he was content, for after so much experiment and theorising, the moment of definite decisions was approaching. The first chain reaction had been achieved in Chicago on December 2, 1942, and it was now to be used to produce a nuclear explosion. The end result was still far off in a mist of conjecture, but at least they had decided on a definite path, or rather a series of paths, to follow. Fuchs' contribution was substantial. He decided to make that contribution, and much else besides, available to the Russians. From this time forward he gave them everything he could, whether it was his own work or not. He brought the answers to their questions; he indicated the success or failure of experiments; and he furnished precise details of dimensions. No one on earth could have made an atomic bomb at that time, and Fuchs then knew little of the United States plans. But he knew nearly all there was to be known about the gas diffusion plant in the Manhattan Engineering District, and that information the Russians got from him.

Throughout his stay in America he had only one contact, and that was Harry Gold, alias "Raymond," the obedient little biochemist who was born in Switzerland and had become a naturalised American. What he did not know was that, through Gold, he was drawn into an elaborate espionage network which had already been working in the United States for some time. Fuchs and the American traitors between them made a nonsense of the security regulations, and they revealed that all the paraphernalia of barbed wire and policemen, unless carried to a stultifying extreme, is a useless barrier in the affairs of the mind. When the atomic bomb came to be exploded, not only Fuchs, but an American traitor as well, were standing inside the barbed wire at Los Alamos, with free access to their courier outside, Harry Gold.

Fuchs proceeded with his tennis ball to the first rendezvous with Gold, on the lower East Side in New York, early in 1944. They met, they proceeded by taxi to a restaurant, and they arranged to meet again. It was Fuchs' practise from this time on to warn Gold in advance of what he proposed to give him at their next meeting; normally it would be a package of papers which he had typed or written himself. He was also prepared to answer questions. Gold, on his side, adopted a system by which, immediately he left Fuchs, he handed over the package to his superior in the net, the Russian Vice Consul in New York, Anatoli A. Yakovlev, who would often be waiting round the corner of the next street—unknown, of course, to Fuchs. Gold then went home—he had a tortuous procedure of jumping on and off trains at the last minute to make sure he was not being followed—and wrote out a report on Fuchs' conversation. This report would be given to Yakovlev at a later, prearranged meeting. In the course of these proceedings Fuchs was once offered $1,500. He turned it down flat.

There were five meetings between Fuchs and Gold in New York, possibly more. In March 1944 they met on Madison Avenue, when they were together less than a minute—just long enough for Fuchs to hand over his papers. They met again in the middle of June at Woodside, Queens, and Fuchs promised that at their next meeting he would bring information of the actual plans for the design of the uranium bomb. At the end of that same month, when they met again near the Brooklyn Borough Hall, he did, in fact, deliver those plans. Gold took them quickly, without waiting to join in conversation. In mid-July they were together again, at 96th Street and Central Park West, and on this occasion they strolled for an hour and a half through the park.

Years afterward, when he was questioned, Fuchs could only remember that his contact "Raymond" was a man who did understand something of the technicalities they discussed. Possibly, he thought, he might have been a chemist. For the most part at this time he passed over his own original manuscripts—which his office supposed he had destroyed after official copies had been made. The main value of this information was that it gave the principles and some details of the gas diffusion production plant at Oak Ridge, Tennessee. He also indicated the scale and timing of the American programme. From his notes the Russians could have deduced the principles of one of the methods we had chosen for separating uranium isotopes, and he could have set at rest their speculations on that score.

At the Central Park meeting they fixed the next rendezvous at the Brooklyn Museum of Art, and, as an alternative—there was always an alternative at a later date in case either of them failed to keep the first appointment—they were to meet again at Central Park West.

But Fuchs failed to keep either of these appointments. It was a matter of concern for the net when an agent vanished in this way, for there was always the possibility that he had been arrested or had decided to cease his activities and had turned traitor to the traitors. Gold's movements then were like those of some agitated insect that has suddenly lost its way. He waited fruitlessly at the meeting place. He went to Fuchs' apartment on 77th Street, but the doorman there could tell him nothing except that Fuchs had gone away. It was Yakovlev who hunted up the address of Fuchs' sister Kristel, and Gold was posted off to Cambridge to see her. Gold explained to her that he was a friend of Fuchs', and wanted rather urgently to see him. Kristel could remember only that Fuchs had gone off "somewhere in the southwest." He had promised to spend the coming Christmas with her if he could. Then, Gold said, would she ask him to telephone when he arrived? He wrote out a New York number and put it in an envelope. Then he went away to report to Yakovlev, and to wait.

What had happened was that Fuchs had been sent to Los Alamos in New Mexico. Professor Peierls and his family had gone there some time before, leaving Fuchs in charge of the

New York office, and now Fuchs himself was wanted to help
on the work for the actual construction of the bomb. It was one
of the quirks of Fuchs' pedantic mind that security should always be observed—at any rate until he chose to break it, in a
way and at a time of his own choosing. Los Alamos was a great
secret. The director, Doctor Robert R. Oppenheimer, was as-
sembling there a group of perhaps the most distinguished scientific minds that has ever been gathered together. Fuchs decided
not to pass on this information to the Russians, nor the news
of his own departure. It was, for the moment, too secret.

He arrived at Los Alamos, was given a room in the bachelors'
dormitory, and there began for him perhaps the happiest time
of his life. Living there, high among the pines, in the clear, dry
air of the desert, he developed a physical well-being that he
could hardly have known before. On his days off he went mountain climbing. In the winter he went skiing. In the sunlight and
the snow most people look rather better than they normally do,
but the photographs taken at this time of Fuchs in his skiing
clothes show that the change was remarkable. He appeared lithe
and assured and good-looking. There was much casual enter-
taining among the families at Los Alamos, and Fuchs frequently
went out dining and dancing. He had more money, and although
money was never a major interest for him, he knew how to spend
it generously and well. Since he loved motoring, Mrs. Peierls
persuaded him to go down to the town of Santa Fe and buy a
car—a secondhand Buick. In every way he seemed more relaxed
and at ease than his friends had ever before known him to be.

The security regulations were not too onerous—and one feels
that Fuchs would not have objected if they had been. At first
the military authorities had wanted to put all the scientists into
uniform, give them ranks, and bring them under Army discipline. At this the scientists objected, and they won their point.
But the military did succeed in ringing them round with barbed

wire; there was one pass to get into the residential camp, and another to visit the laboratories and offices, and the guards on the gate were punctilious. Once inside the camp, conversation among the scientists and their families was free and easy, but the pass system was formidable, and the townspeople down at Santa Fe had no notion of what was going on up there on the bare heights above. They believed, as Harry Gold expressively put it in court much later, that it was a "sort of boondoggling outfit." Still, the scientists could and did go to Santa Fe, and it was always possible for them to get tickets of leave.

Early in 1945, after six months of this life of engrossing work in the fresh air, Fuchs went east to spend a short holiday with his sister Kristel Heineman and her family in Cambridge, and there the faithful Harry Gold appeared. He came first to the Heineman flat, and asked Fuchs about his work at Los Alamos. Fuchs agreed to put down all he knew in writing, and this material was handed over to Gold at a second meeting in a Boston street a few days later.

By now Fuchs was able to reveal a great deal. In his notes he gave details of the plutonium bomb (as distinct from the uranium bomb), its design, the method of construction, and the fact that the plutonium was produced in atomic piles at Hanford in the state of Washington. In particular, he gave a description of an implosion lens (a device that explodes inward) which was to be used in detonating the plutonium bomb. Later the Russians evinced much interest in this implosion lens; they pressed Gold to scour his mind for any further details Fuchs may have given him, and in the end Gold succeeded in getting actual drawings of the lens from the American traitor David Greenglass, who was also working in Los Alamos.

Before Fuchs and Gold parted in Boston it was agreed that they should have a further meeting in the summer and that it should take place at Santa Fe since it was unlikely that Fuchs would be able to come east again. The place was to be the Castillo Bridge in Santa Fe, and the time was to be six months later at 4 P.M. on the first Saturday in June 1945—June 2.

Looking back now, Fuchs' friends can remember that he returned from Boston at the end of February, after ten days' absence, looking harassed and depressed. He offered no explanation beyond saying that he was worried about his sister.

The June meeting took place precisely as arranged. Gold came from New York by train. Wary as ever, he bought a map of Santa Fe so that he could find his way to the Castillo Bridge without enquiring of anyone, and a few minutes after 4 Fuchs appeared in his Buick. They were together barely half an hour. Fuchs handed over another batch of papers. He said that there had been tremendous progress and that the first atomic explosion would definitely take place in the Alamogordo desert during the following month. They fixed the next meeting at 6 P.M. on September 19, near a church on a road leading out of Santa Fe, and Fuchs drove off to Los Alamos. Gold then took a bus to Albuquerque, sixty miles away, and there had an interview with his other contact at Los Alamos, David Greenglass. It was then that Greenglass gave him the drawings of the implosion lens. It must have been one of the most profitable journeys Gold or any other Russian agent ever made.

When President Truman met Stalin at Potsdam the following month, and told him that the American and British scientists had developed a new kind of bomb far more destructive than anything known before and that it would be dropped on Japan unless she surrendered, Stalin manifested nothing more than polite interest and said that he hoped the bomb would be used. He made no attempt to enquire further, or follow up the conversation in any way. No doubt he was aware that his Director of Intelligence in Moscow had already a full account of the making of the bomb, based on the information of Fuchs, Greenglass,

Nunn May, and others. There are grounds for believing that, at the time, the Russians made no use of this painfully gathered information. They had their own eminent scientists in Russia, but they, like many scientists in Europe, may not have believed the project to be possible; nor had they yet made use of the Nazi scientists who had been captured at the fall of Germany in May. It seems hard to believe that Stalin's nonchalance was due to either indifference or incredulity. With the prospect of a third World War before them, in the series of "frightful clashes" which Lenin had predicted, it is also very difficult to believe that Russian Intelligence could have failed to pass on their information to the Politburo and emphasize its importance. Yet such things can happen. At all events, no more was said at the time at Potsdam, and Gouzenko's defection from the Soviet Embassy at Ottawa—which eventually brought the whole matter into the open—did not happen until a fortnight later.

Meanwhile, the first atomic bomb was exploded in the Alamogordo desert on July 16, 1945. Let us follow the adventures of Fuchs on that momentous day. For him, and for so many others at Los Alamos who had worked upon this single project for so many years and with so little hope in the beginning, there was an excitement and a tension that was almost past bearing.

On the previous day Professor Peierls, Fuchs, and others were assigned to one of the military buses, and drove off to the scene. Being theorists, who were not concerned with the actual work of exploding the bomb, the party was directed to a position on rising ground some twenty miles away from the tower on which the bomb was erected. They were on the spot before midnight, and the bomb was timed to go off in the early hours of the morning so that there would be the advantage of taking night photographs, and of observing the explosive light against the background of the darkness. Each man was equipped with dark glasses and was under instructions to lie down when he

saw the flash. It was necessary that there should be no rain
and that the wind should be blowing from the right quarter
so that the radioactive dust should be carried into the empty
desert.

It seemed that these conditions had been fulfilled, when,
shortly before zero hour, word came through on the field tele-
phones that a technical hitch had occurred and there would be
a delay. There was nothing that Fuchs or the other theoretical
physicists could do about this; they had made their calculations
and checked them many times over. They had proved on paper
that if the bomb were constructed and detonated in a certain way
it must explode. The making of the bomb and the actual experiment—with all the possibility of mechanical error—were beyond their province.

It was on the point of getting light, and they were about to
accept a postponement until the following night, when an
enormous flash filled the sky. It was far brighter than anything
they had expected. Its form and colouring they had anticipated
—the white column rising to an orange ball, and the purple
shade created by the ozone above—but all this was monstrously
and unexpectedly bright. Some flung themselves on the ground.
Fuchs and others remained standing. This was the end of their
years of work.

There was no wind and no sound, and this absence of sound
seemed unnatural and frightening. They remained fixed in their
positions until at last there was a little crack—rather like a
distant rifle shot. It was so mild a thing, compared to the awe-
some and expanding light, that one of the party who was not a
scientist asked incredulously, "What was that?" as though, after
this long interval of silence, it was remarkable that the explosion
should make any sound at all.

The party got back into the bus and drove toward Albuquerque, two hours away. They were exhausted, and in their

natural reaction to the past excitement, their one thought was
breakfast. At Albuquerque, however, they were told that orders
had been issued that they were not to stop, lest the townspeople
should see the elation in their faces. Glumly the party continued
for another three hours to Los Alamos, where their families
appeared to be fully informed about what had happened in the
night. One scientist who was ill declared he saw the flash from
his bed in the camp hospital. Alamogordo was 150 miles away.

The Alamogordo explosion was the beginning of the end of
Anglo-American association over the atomic bomb. It was
dropped on Hiroshima by the American Air Force August 6,
1945, and on Nagasaki August 9; and six days later the war
against Japan was over. The British scientists began winding
up their affairs in the United States, and in September a farewell
party of more than normal scope was arranged. No liquor was
sold in the Los Alamos camp, nor indeed was any supposed to
be brought in, but it was not a rule that was enforced too
rigorously, especially now that the war was over. Fuchs went
down to Santa Fe to buy the whisky. He was hours late in
returning—so late that his friends thought he must have had an
accident, or that the guard had discovered the liquor in the car.
When he finally arrived he was somewhat taciturn, and merely
said, without explanation, that he had been delayed. He had
indeed "been delayed," for this was September 19, and in addition to buying the whisky he had been talking to Harry Gold.

They had met, as they had arranged, by the church on the
road leading out of Santa Fe, and this, their last, was a long
meeting. Fuchs had written down all he knew. He gave the size
of the bomb—a vital point—what it contained, how it was constructed, and how it was detonated. He gave his own calculations of the actual dimensions of the parts. And he handed all
this over in a package to Gold. He also talked. He spoke with
awe of the explosion and the excitement it had caused. Its flash

had been visible two hundred miles away, and now that the
secret of the Los Alamos camp was out, the local townspeople
regarded the scientists as heroes. But there was no longer, he
said, the same free and easy co-operation between the Americans
and the British. Now security regulations had come into force,
and a number of the departments were closed to him. He had
been told that he would soon have to return to the United
Kingdom.

He said he was troubled about his return. There was a possibility that his father, Doctor Fuchs, who had survived the war
in Germany, might visit him in England, and there was a danger
that the old man might talk about his son's connection with the
Communist Party in Germany in his student days. Furthermore,
it was very worrying that it was the British and not the Russians
who had captured Kiel. There was a Gestapo dossier on him at
Kiel, and it would be awkward if it fell into the hands of British
Intelligence, for that dossier would reveal that he had been a
leader of the Communist student group, and had fought the
Nazi storm troopers in the streets of Kiel.

But he was prepared, nevertheless, to continue his espionage
for Russia. These were the arrangements he agreed upon with
Gold for making contact again on his return to England:

Beginning on the first Saturday of every month after his return, Fuchs was to be at the street entrance of the Paddington
Crescent underground station* in London at 8 P.M. He was to
be carrying five books, bound with string, and supported by two
fingers of one hand; in the other hand he was to be holding
two more books. His contact, whoever it might be, was to be
carrying a book by Bennett Cerf, *Try and Stop Me*.

Fuchs was one of the last of the British scientists to leave Los
Alamos. Long after Professor Peierls had gone he continued
as chief of the dwindling British team to write his reports on

* There is no Paddington Crescent station. Possibly Mornington Crescent
was meant.

the work of the previous two years in America. Before this he
had already been offered the post of head of the Theoretical
Physics Division at the new British atomic energy centre at
Harwell in Berkshire. The salary was £1200 a year, rising to
£1800. He was commended everywhere for his work in the
United States, and security in particular was full of praise for
his caution. He had arrived now at the front rank.

In the eight months that elapsed between his last meeting
with Harry Gold in Santa Fe and his departure from Los Alamos
in June 1946, Fuchs made no attempt to get in touch with the
Russians, or they with him. Gouzenko's defection in Ottawa
occurred on September 5, 1945, and there seems to have followed a long quietus in the activities of the Russian Intelligence
Service all over the world. It seems likely that the Director in
Moscow called a halt, or at any rate a slowing down, until it
should be known just how far the Canadian enquiry was going
to go. Then, too, traitors as well as everybody else suffered from
the general feeling of inertia that succeeded the war; there was
no longer the same urgency. Nor were there as many secrets.

Toward the end of November 1945, Fuchs made a brief visit
to Montreal and Chicago on official business—it was on this trip
that he was interviewed for his Harwell appointment. In the
following month he drove with the Peierls on a motoring holiday to Mexico. He was unimpressed, as always, by the tourist
sights, but the Peierls noticed that there was something also
which was strange in his manner. He was more abstracted than
usual. It seems possible that in Mexico—one of the regular stag-
ing posts for Communist agents—he may have contemplated
continuing on to Russia. But he came back to the United States
with the Peierls, and then, on June 16 of the next year, he left
Los Alamos for the last time. He travelled first to Washington,
and then continued north for a final visit to his sister in Cambridge on June 21. On June 28 he left Montreal by air for
England.

Nine

•

A RECENT GUIDEBOOK PUBLISHED IN ENGLAND* CONTAINS THE
following note on Harwell:

Post-war Berkshire's crowning state monument is Harwell Atomic
Research Establishment. It was built on the downs by order of the
Ministry of Supply, which overrode other ministries and local objec-
tions. It drains labour from the nearby agricultural villages; its im-
ported workers swell the old towns of Wantage and Abingdon to
impracticable size. Its prefabs and factories spread monthly farther
over the downs and higher into the skyline. Its service to Berkshire is
that the scientists in it are engaged in splitting the material of which
the world and its inhabitants are made.

In the original village of Harwell itself, the centre of a cherry-
growing district, there is a 14th century church in which comic
figures in stone can be observed being bitten by dragons. The
Research Establishment, the guidebook goes on, "is fortunately
out of sight of this attractive village and much nearer Chilton,
about two miles away to the south-west."

Sir John Cockcroft, the first scientist in charge, wrote:

We were given Harwell on a windy day of February 1946 on a flying
visit from Canada. There was much transatlantic cabling on where

* *Murray's Berkshire Architectural Guide,* edited by John Betjeman and
John Piper.

we should establish housing sites. A start had to be made quickly, and the only solution was to provide prefabs and to erect them on our own site where services and sewers were available and where the minimum of consents had to be obtained.

The guidebook goes on:

The result is a sudden muddle, worse than the Slough Trading Estate, and enclosed in a high wire fence, with a huge brick chimney, box-like factories and spreading prefabs and hundreds of buses waiting on acres of windy asphalt. It dominates the downs (and these were originally scheduled against building) for miles. Sir John Cockcroft admits that "something might have been better done had we more time for thought and less separation of space in the planning stage."

On a moonlight night the thatch and tile, stone and brick, elms and barns and farms of Old Harwell village compared with the blue electric glare and bright sinister workshops of the Atomic Research Establishment form an instructive contrast between the past and present.

Not far off is the famous White Horse of Uffington, an outline drawing which was cut out of the green turf in the Iron Age, about 100 B.C. The horse is associated with magical pagan rites of the Druids, and St. George is supposed to have killed the dragon there.

The guidebook description of Harwell is a little unfair, because it was written at a time when the station was still under construction. Since then a great deal has been done by the planting of lawns and gardens to bring the place more into harmony with the landscape, and the modern red brickwork is slowly weathering into the native colours of Berkshire.*

Yet there is something a little menacing and forbidding in the air. You come up to Harwell on an ordinary "A" class coun-

---

* It should be remembered that the ensuing paragraphs were written in 1951. Harwell has changed somewhat since then.

try road from Oxford, and the first thing you notice is a wire fence with warning signs hanging on it. There is a copy of the Official Secrets Act on the front gate, and close by is the police guard. There are many police at Harwell.

It is built on the site of a wartime airfield, from which airborne forces took off in gliders on D Day in 1944 for the invasion of Normandy. There are no surrounding houses; the buildings stand in isolation on a large flat plateau, and beyond them there is nothing much to be seen but the green, empty slopes of the downs. The residential quarters are composed partly of RAF houses, built during the war (Sir John Cockcroft himself lived in a rectangular, three-story brick house once occupied by the RAF Station commandant), staff hostels, and two recently constructed villages of standard aluminum prefabricated houses that look like enlarged rabbit hutches. These villages are placed on either side of the airfield. The main site—the actual laboratories and office blocks—stands between them, enclosed by the security fence. Recently the gardeners of the Ministry of Works have planted diligently, and in the late summer it is a pleasant thing on coming through the front gate (your pass gripped in your hand) to see the English lawns, the beds of zinnias, dahlias, roses, and chrysanthemums.

As far as possible the old RAF hangars have been employed, with the wartime camouflage still fading on their walls. A new use has been found for the RAF watertower; more and more buildings are going up, and the whole place looks not unlike a California movie studio, but very neat and new and tidy. From inside one peers through the wire fence at the deserted asphalt runways, which are now gradually breaking up, with tufts of grass starting through them, and beyond that are the cows grazing in the open countryside.

The older village of prefabricated houses is set in a shallow horseshoe on the side of a green slope, with lawns in front of all the

houses. Each flat-topped, greyish-white hut has some attempt
at a little garden: a few vegetables, a clothesline at the back,
and here and there a baby's pram on the front porch. These
houses are identical—a living room, two bedrooms, a kitchen, a
bathroom—and are so small that when the WC is used the whole
house is aware of it. Fuchs lived in No. 17 at the end of one row.

The administrative block is the first building inside the en-
closure, a low, two-story structure; and there Fuchs latterly had
his office, close to Sir John Cockcroft and the security officers.
It is a light and airy place, lit by glass domes in the roof, and
in working hours it is no different from any other English
office. Secretaries and young men pass by along the corridors
bearing cups of tea and files of papers. On the notice boards
nothing more unusual appears than advertisements about national savings schemes, perhaps a newspaper cutting of a car-
toonist's joke about the atomic bomb ("Up Boys and Atom"),
or even possibly an announcement that the Metallurgical Ball
will be held at the Village Hall on Saturday night, tickets 7/6d,
obtainable from any member of the metallurgical staff.

These things, however, are in very great contrast to the atomic
pile itself, and that to a layman is as strange as any dragon, or
any magical rite practised by the Druids in the Iron Age on
White Horse Hill. It is a massive thing, in shape somewhat re-
sembling the reconstruction of the Mausoleum of Halicarnassus,
and it is tended by men in white overalls. There is no dust, no
noise, no hurrying, and no disorder. A clinical calm covers all, and
on a first visit it is difficult to avoid feeling unnaturally alert and
wary, as though one were entering some unexplored cavern,
from which wild beasts might suddenly pounce out. One half
expects the whole thing to blow up.

Across the wide, clean concrete floor of the building men go
by like sailors on the deck of a ship. There are many notices
saying "Danger" and "Radio-active waste"; and the words "Neu-

tron Ray Trap" are painted on the side of a concrete cube which is intended to block some vent, which reaches, like a dragon's throat, into the centre of the pile. In one quarter men are packing and dispatching containers of isotopes which are used in hospitals. Others are manning compressed-air pumps that drive the rods of uranium into the pile. Stacks of graphite lie about, looking like loaves of black bread. Large cranes reach down from above, and in the control room there is a wide arc of lighted dials, which reminds one of the cockpit of an aeroplane, immensely magnified—or possibly the bridge of a ship. Most remarkable of all, there is a notice with red lettering strung high above your head and this reads, "No Smoking on Top of the Pile"—as though one might say, "No Lighting of Matches in the Crater of the Volcano."

After a little, you overcome your fear; an engineer will explain all the many safeguards against explosion—making his points on a transparent model of the pile—and you believe him. You can advance, if you wish, to the pile itself and touch it. You can pick up a rod of uranium in your hand. The notice about smoking is explained. It has no importance any more; it was put there simply to prevent workmen from dropping their cigarette butts into the graphite while the pile was being built, since the graphite must be as pure as possible. In other words, the impediment is not smoke but dirt and no normal earthly heat could affect this experiment.

The "hot" laboratory is more strange than the pile itself, for here men work like divers, in rubber boots and gloves; and when they emerge from their work to the uncontaminated air, they step into transparent cubicles not unlike a telephone booth, to be sprayed with citric acid. They may not touch objects inside the laboratory; as they advance toward a door they cut a photo-electric ray, and the door opens of itself. This building is constructed on the same principles (though not perhaps with the

same grace) as the Doge's Palace in Venice, with all the mass
of masonry at the top and the windows below. The whole of
the second storey is filled with brightly coloured machinery, for
sucking out the radioactive air from the laboratories below. This
air is roasted and purified, and then released harmlessly through
a tall chimney into the Berkshire sky. Outside, there are radioactive water tanks where the water also is purified before it is
returned to the River Thames and the sea. The waste from the
experiments is collected in movable concrete buckets, which are
eventually dumped into the ocean.

The people at Harwell have long since accepted with equa-
nimity this contamination they create, and the latent danger, as
one presumably grows accustomed to heights, or to the diseases
that are gathered in a hospital. Every member of the staff is
regularly given an X-ray test and a medical examination to gauge
his reaction to the radioactive atmosphere, and the safeguards
are such that no one has been affected yet. But the visitor will
find out how thin is his own façade of assurance, if, as he is
standing by the pile, there is some sudden noise—someone drops
a girder or there is a blast from the compressed-air pump. Then
he will jump. Then his imagination will remind him that the
end result of this work could be the annihilation of the world.
And he is not reassured when he is told that the atomic bomb
is only a small part of the study of nuclear fission, that already
the hospitals are being greatly helped, and that the wasted heat
generated in the pile is being put to practical use in heating
the laboratories in the winter.

Outside their work, the staff at Harwell have as much opportunity to live a normal life as the members of any other engineering community in Berkshire. They pass freely in and out of the
security fence; many of them in fact live in Abingdon, and other
towns some miles away. They have their tennis courts, their
schools, their holidays, and their Metallurgical Ball. They are

not divided from the rest of society except only in this—having signed the Official Secrets Act, it is up to them to be wary in their conversation. And this does create a strain for in a natural state most men do not enjoy keeping secrets any more than they prefer to keep money unused in the bank. They prefer to spend.

Their conditions of domestic living are unexciting and unexceptional. They have their canteen at Harwell, and they converge there each day—rather pale and thinnish young men, with a student seriousness—to eat a meal of soup, meat, and vegetables, and perhaps a slice of sponge cake with a little coloured jelly on top, which is the normal thing in British canteens, unappetising to a foreign eye, but not injurious. Their conversation is garrison conversation, and not markedly different from the usual run of such conversation in canteens all over England: the weather, football, the news, holidays, and—when by themselves—their work. In short, they are remarkable only for their ability as scientists, engineers, and chemists, for their integrity, and for their interest in their work. Quite aside from the moral issues, it would not be possible for them to become traitors, for that would destroy the life by which they live, their work, and everything they ever believed in. Harwell has become a tradition for the scientists now. It has a routine, solid buildings, and a local loyalty, and it is as firmly established as any institution is ever likely to be in 20th century Europe.

But when Fuchs arrived, in July 1946, fresh from his success in America, all this was just beginning. Work had been started on the new buildings barely six months before, and Harwell was still an airfield on a windy hilltop. Fuchs was brought in to help on the original planning, and he had all the mixed joys of starting something from the beginning. He staffed his own division of theoretical physicists, he gave the orders for their work, and to some extent he fixed the programme. In the end a part of Harwell was his own creation.

He lived at first in the bachelors' quarters of the staff club, which was inexpensive. When he heard that there was a feeling in Harwell that the staff club should be reserved for junior and lower-salaried members of the staff, he moved to a boarding-house at Abingdon, five or six miles away, and remained there for two and a half years. Prefabricated houses in the encampment were set aside for married couples. As the head of a division, however, Fuchs was eventually given one of these, and in 1948 he moved from Abingdon into No. 17. Soon he got rid of his dilapidated 8 h.p. Morris, and bought from a colleague a grey saloon MG car; on his salary of about £1500 he could live more expansively than before. He began to make friends, mostly among senior members of the staff, and notably Professor and Mrs. W. H. B. Skinner, and the Senior Security Officer, Wing Commander Henry Arnold, and his wife.

Once or twice he went abroad. He took one holiday with Professor and Mrs. Peierls in Switzerland, and another in the south of France and along the Mediterranean with Professor and Mrs. Skinner. On the Swiss holiday he went to Saas-Fé, near Zermatt, where the Peierls had taken an apartment; and it was here that he met Gerhardt, his elder brother, who came over from Davos for a couple of days. They had not met since before the war. Gerhardt was totally unlike Klaus—he had grown very fat, he was very feeble, and life was already ebbing away from him. The two brothers spent a long time talking together alone.

In November 1947, when Klaus had been at Harwell nearly eighteen months, he flew to Washington for a declassification conference. This was attended by representatives of the United States, Canada, and Britain, and the object of the meeting was to examine the atomic knowledge shared by the three countries in the war, and to decide what should or should not be published. No knowledge which the three countries had acquired independently since the war was discussed. This conference took place in Washington from November 14 to 16—Friday, Saturday, and Sunday. Fuchs was a member of a subcommittee which specifically considered the Los Alamos period, and he is remembered as being generally conservative on the release of information.*

While in America on this trip he paid a short visit to the Argonne Laboratory in Chicago to discuss neutron spectroscopy, but, on the instructions of United States security, he saw nothing that was secret. The visit lasted only an hour and forty minutes.

In England Fuchs often went up to London for conferences at the Ministry of Supply. It was sometimes the practise of the Harwell scientists who attended these meetings to stay on in London for a few hours to do their shopping or go to the theatre or a cinema. Fuchs never accompanied them. On the other hand, he did not take an early train back to Harwell. He returned alone on the late train from Paddington, often bringing with him some small present for the wives of his friends at Harwell. His consideration for his friends at this time, his many kindnesses, did not seem to them then to be anything else than the expression of a genuine affection. Nor have they altered their opinion since. During these years of his middle 30's Fuchs was not perhaps a companionable man, but he developed a warmth and an ease of manner that was something new. He did not entertain very much; after his arrest his charwoman remarked that he ate his meals at the staff club, and the "prefab" was nothing much more than a bachelor's bungalow. But she found him a pleasant man.

He still showed no signs whatever of getting married, but he had friends among the scientists' wives, and he discussed with

---

* Later, however, he worked out an elaborate scheme of declassification—possibly with the idea of establishing that the information he had given the Russians was no longer secret.

them eagerly the prospect of his nephew coming to live with him. In 1947 he gave Mrs. Peierls a blank cheque so that she could buy clothes for his father on the first visit to England. Then again in 1949 he helped Doctor Fuchs with his expenses on a visit to the United States, and he entertained him at Abingdon on his return. His Quaker friends remember meeting Klaus about this time—the summer of 1949—and asking him if he still held to his left-wing views. He replied that he had given them up entirely. The Russians were intractable. The only hope now was to form a close alliance of the Western democracies.

Among the scientists at Harwell he never talked politics. They knew him simply as a man with an obsession for his work. In committee meetings he sat silently through most of the discussions, and when he was asked for his opinion he gave it precisely and clearly, in the manner of someone who has already delved deep into the matter and has firmly made up his mind. He had his occasional fits of illness, his drinking, his incessant smoking of cigarettes, but all the rest was work. He presided like a housemaster over the Harwell welfare committee, and he had a housemaster's convinced pride in the affairs of the whole establishment. Had there been Harwell colours and a school tie, Fuchs would have worn them.

That was his outward life. During these three years—from 1946 to 1949—his secret life was performing new and unpredictable evolutions of its own. He did not keep the rendezvous so carefully made for him at Mornington Crescent Underground station, nor any of the alternative appointments. On their side the Russians made no attempt to approach him or renew the contact in any way. The obvious though not perhaps the complete explanation is that Gouzenko had defected in September 1945 and the Russian Intelligence Service was lying low until they saw what came out of it. Fuchs, like Nunn May, may have considered washing his hands of the whole business on his re-

turn from the United States. Certainly the risks were much
greater now that Nunn May had been discovered; and, in any
event, at Harwell Fuchs had much less to tell the Russians than
he had had at Los Alamos.

So he continued for a year in England, without making a
move. Early in 1947,* like a drug addict who had mastered his
mania for a time and then suddenly succumbs again, Fuchs
went in search of the Communist who had originally put him
in touch with Simon Kremer six years before. He failed to find
him, but in the course of his enquiries he found a woman Party
member who was willing to help.

This woman introduced him to the Russians in London, and
the drug began to work again. Soon he received instructions to go
to a public house in north London. He was to go into the saloon
bar carrying a copy of the weekly paper *Tribune* and take a seat
on a certain bench. His contact would carry a red book.

Fuchs went and found his man. The meeting opened unfavour-
ably; Fuchs was berated for re-establishing contact through a
known member of the Communist Party. Henceforth he was
to steer entirely clear of all known Communists. This scolding
may have added to his feeling of guilt at having deserted the
Russians for so long, and may go some way toward explaining
what he did next. He accepted a gift of £100 in bank notes.
Up to this time he had rejected any payment, except small sums
(mainly from Harry Gold in the United States) to cover his
expenses in getting to and from his places of rendezvous. But this
£100 was different—far too much for his expenses on an occasional trip from Harwell to London, and not nearly enough
to compensate for the value of his treason, as to make espionage
a really profitable undertaking. Fuchs himself says that he took
the money as a symbol, as a formal act to bind himself to the

---

* This was just after he had met his Communist brother Gerhardt in
Switzerland.

cause. After this there could be no going back: he had taken money and he was committed forever. That is his explanation; and since he is the only witness of his own thoughts, it must be noted, if not accepted. He took no more money from the Russians after this.

There began now in 1947 a new series of eight meetings over the next two years, usually at intervals of two or three months, and always with the same man. The meetings were in London, and in either one of two public houses—the Spotted Horse in High Street, Putney, or the Nag's Head at Wood Green. If for some reason one of the two conspirators failed to appear, then it was understood they should meet precisely a week later at the same place. Should the rendezvous fail a second time, then they would meet at the alternative public house a month later. If once again this failed, they would come back again to this second public house the following week.

In 1948 they made a further arrangement in case all these appointments should go wrong: Fuchs would go to a private house in Richmond which was pointed out to him on one of his London trips and there throw a periodical over the fence. He was to write a message on the tenth page. They had one more arrangement, to be used if either of them wished to indicate in advance that he could not keep an appointment: they would chalk a cross at an agreed spot near the Kew Gardens railway station.

However, in the event the meetings seem to have succeeded admirably. Fuchs came up from Harwell (possibly on those days when he had official committees to attend at the Ministry of Supply in Shell-Mex House in the Strand) and slipped off to his appointment in the early evening. He and his contact never made a signal of recognition when they met in the saloon bar. Instead, they would walk out into the street independently, and then stroll along together while Fuchs handed over his information. Sometimes the contact would leave Fuchs standing in the street for ten minutes or so, and then come back and resume his questioning; clearly, another man (who kept out of Fuchs' sight) was being consulted.

There cannot have been a great deal that Fuchs gave the Russians during this period. He was cut off from nearly all the secret American research that had been continued after the war, and Harwell was still in its early stages. But he gave them various details of the British plutonium piles at Windscale, in Cumberland, and he gave figures of American production up to the time he left Los Alamos. It was at this time that the Russians pressed him for information about the hydrogen bomb, but Fuchs could have given them little more than the principles that had been discussed at Los Alamos.

Now that they were making their own bombs, the Russians were avid for anything they could get; once they even urged Fuchs to go to Paris and make contact there at a certain address with other agents who had a technical knowledge of his work. But this he refused to do. It was by now late in 1948, and his erratic conscience was about to take one more epochal decision on behalf of mankind. He was beginning to have doubts about the Russians. Worse still, he began to detect a new weakness in himself: an attachment to Harwell, an unwillingness to go on cheating his friends there indefinitely. In this twilight stage, when for once his conscience did not point the right way ahead with a clear, burning light, he found himself drifting into a compromise—a thing he would never have done in the bright, certain days of Los Alamos, when the double life was so easy to live and everything was either black or white. He decided not to break with the Russians altogether, but gradually to give them less and less while his conscience wrestled with this problem, until it gave him a new lead one way or the other.

Fuchs has himself explained the process:

In the course of this work I began naturally to form bonds of personal friendship, and I had to conceal them from my inner thoughts. I used my Marxist philosophy to establish in my mind two separate compartments: one compartment in which I allowed myself to make friendships, to have personal relations, to help people, and to be in all personal ways the kind of man I wanted to be, and the kind of man, which, in a personal way, I had been before with my friends in or near the Communist Party. I could be free and easy and happy with other people without fear of disclosing myself, because I knew that the other compartment would step in if I approached the danger point. I could forget the other compartment and still rely upon it. It appeared to me at the time that I had become a "free man," because I had succeeded in the other department in establishing myself completely independent of the surrounding forces of society. Looking back on it now, the best way of expressing it seems to be to call it a controlled schizophrenia.

In the postwar period I began again to have my doubts about the Russian policy. It is impossible to give definite incidents, because now the control mechanism acted against me also, in keeping away from me facts which I could not look in the face; but they did penetrate, and eventually I came to the point where I knew I disapproved of many actions of the Russian Government and of the Communist Party, but I still believed that they would build a new world and that one day I would take part in it, and that on that day I would also have to stand up and say to them that there are things which they are doing wrongly. During this time I was not sure that I could give all the information that I had. However, it became more and more evident that the time when Russia would expand her influence over Europe was far away, and that therefore I had to decide for myself whether I could go on for many years to continue handing over information without being sure in my own mind whether I was doing right. I decided that I could not do so. I did not go to one rendezvous because I was ill at the time. I decided not to go to the following one.

There have been evidences of insanity in all the members of Fuchs' family except his father and mother. This passage quoted from his confession is not insanity, but there is a megalomania in it: "I had to decide for myself. . . . I decided . . . I decided." He is not only deciding for himself but for society as well; he is the judge, the prosecution, the witness, and the executioner all rolled into one. And then there is the glory of being the "free man"—the superman who is above the normal rules of the community, who has perfectly pigeonholed his emotions and his duties. He keeps, as it were, a watchdog in the private background of his life, and this dog is entirely reliable and trustworthy, the devoted guardian—until one day it inexplicably turns round and begins to bite him.

It is a strange mixture, but it is not unknown in insane asylums. In some ways, however, the asylum case is simpler than Klaus Fuchs. The poor, frustrated creature who thinks he is Napoleon, or who defiantly heaves a brick through a window in order to show that he has the power to do such a thing, is an uncontrolled schizophrenic. Quite simply he cannot help doing what he does; and when his fit has passed and he again submits himself to the warder and the rules of society, he cannot understand the reason for his moment of grandeur and frenzy, and he is ashamed.

But even in his calmer moments Fuchs is not ashamed—or at any rate he was not in 1948. He did not acknowledge the existence of a warder, or of any controlling force outside himself. Everything came from within himself, Klaus Fuchs. *He* decided. Not even Marx and the Russians were infallible, or competent to control him, for now he says he will have to stand up to the Russians and tell them they were wrong.

His father, Doctor Emil Fuchs, also had the courage to stand up and tell people where they were wrong. But Doctor Fuchs acknowledged a power that was greater than himself, his God, and he was obedient to God and the Christian principles, which were not of his own making. Klaus Fuchs never had that faith outside himself; he was never obedient to Karl Marx or to any-body.

There may be features of this mentality which are common to most men at some time in their lives: that desire for rightness, the adolescent dream of a world that is perfectly pure and good, and oneself a shining hero in it. Equally, in moments of frustration or bravado (which is frustration in action), few men have not felt the craving to heave a brick through a window just to establish that they are not midgets in the world, not people to be lightly neglected, not cowards anyway. It is the peculiarity of Fuchs that he carried these adolescent emotions on into adult life; and by the accident of his splendid mathematical mind there was put into his hand an enormous brick, with the possibility of his heaving it through an enormous window. His knowledge of the atomic bomb made him a king for a moment, with the fate of mankind in his hand. And all the conspiratorial business of tennis balls and chalk crosses and meetings in pubs must have given the drama a certain schoolboy relish.

But now, in 1948, some ten years too late, the thing that Fuchs had not bargained for begins to happen. He begins to feel the stirrings of attachment to the ordinary, fallible human beings around him—the things that have come his way through the pure accident of time and politics and geography. There are his friends at Harwell, the Skinners, the Arnolds, his friends Professor Peierls and his wife. He begins to think that he might owe them a duty, too, even though that duty may conflict with his larger design of creating a perfect world. There is his department at Harwell, all the work that has yet to be done. Perhaps there might be claims on him there, too. Perhaps the immediate world around him might have some call on his loyalty, and some return ought to be made for the ordinary, simple affection of the people who have known and trusted him these last few years. He begins to feel that he needs that affection. And, finally, it is even

possible that something is due to England itself since he has
accepted its hospitality for so long and has indeed grown to
depend on it.

The business of growing up when one is an adult already is
never easy, and for Fuchs it was a torment. An incident occurred
about this time—August 1948—when Fuchs was tapering off the
information he was giving the Russians, and it reveals something of the strain under which he lived. Nothing was thought
of this incident at the time, but it was remembered later with
interest. A Mr. S. M. Duke of Harwell had been attending a
meeting at the General Electric Company at Wembley, outside
London, with Fuchs and one or two other colleagues. When
the meeting was over Duke asked if anyone would like a lift
back to Harwell in his car. Fuchs accepted and sat next to Duke
on the front seat. They began the journey in daylight, around
five in the afternoon, and had reached a spot on the Oxford
Road between Gerrards Cross and Beaconsfield when some object suddenly struck the windscreen with a sharp report. The
glass cracked into tiny pieces and became opaque. The car was
then travelling about forty miles an hour, and Duke, unable to
see where he was going, knocked out the windscreen with his
hand while he braked as hard as he could. Fuchs slid off the
seat onto the floor under the dashboard, and there was a look
of extreme fear in his face, as though he had been seized by a
heart attack.

When the car came to a standstill Fuchs remained where he
was. Duke got out of the car and began picking out the remaining bits of broken glass, remarking that a stone must have flown
up from the roadway. Fuchs would not accept this explanation
at all. He pointed out that the road surface was clean, smooth
tarmac, and that no other car could have thrown up a stone
since there was no other traffic on the road. He spoke excitedly,
and it was plain that he was badly shaken. He would not get

out of the car until an Automobile Association patrol and others arrived.

It was then discovered that some of the pieces of broken glass showed traces of lead streaks, which could have come from an uncoated bullet fired from a .22 rifle or revolver. Since he had heard no bang, Duke was inclined to think that it was a bullet fired from some distance off—possibly a ricochet from the rifle of somebody who was out after rabbits. Equally, it might have been a piece of lead projected from a boy's catapult. Fuchs was not reassured, and they completed the journey home in great discomfort, while the rain poured in on them.

It seems inconceivable that anyone tried to murder Fuchs that day, for he was not travelling in his own car, he had accepted the lift with Duke quite by chance, and this was not the only route between Wembley and Harwell. But clearly, for a moment, he thought he had been shot at, and the self-control on which he had prided himself for so long deserted him.

Then his illness intervened. He went down to the Mediterranean on holiday with the Skinners in the spring of 1949, and he was not very well on the journey. When he got back, it developed that he had a spot on one lung, which—he says—made him miss one of his London appointments. Mrs. Skinner nursed him in her own house at Harwell. This was one of the times when he lay staring at the wall without eating or speaking; he persisted in remaining in bed after his illness had gone, and it was no longer necessary for him to stay indoors. These unrecorded hours, when he struggled with his perplexed loyalties, when he hunted and hunted through his mind for some clear answer, were probably the crisis of Fuchs' existence—the death throes, as it were, of his private life. When he got up at last, he had resolved to break with the Russians. He would not confess; that opened up possibilities that were too frightful. But from now on he would live one life instead of two: he would give his allegiance to Harwell, his work, and his friends, and Russia would have to shift the best she could for herself. He could not repent: he had done all he had done with a clear moral conscience. But in the future he would live the easier life, where what he said and did openly would be at one with his thoughts.

There could have been circumstances in which Fuchs might possibly have escaped detection by that decision. Conceivably he might have accomplished a genuine conversion and then have died, without anyone ever being the wiser about his treason. But it so happened that it was too late. In the summer of 1949 an investigation had already begun. And on September 1 President Truman made an announcement in Washington which meant that neither traitors nor anyone else were going to sleep quite securely in their beds for some time to come, if ever at all. Russia had exploded her first atomic bomb.

Ten

•

THE SECURITY SYSTEM IN ENGLAND HAS BEEN AN EMPIRICAL GROWTH; it has developed piecemeal over the centuries as the need for it arose, and there has never been a moment when by one sweeping administrative act some central body like the FBI in the United States was established. Instead there is a network of security agencies.

In England there is no great reverence for security officials, or much belief in the efficiency of "loyalty" tests. On the other hand, there is no great record of treason either. Something like three hundred years have passed since the last civil war, and successive governments since then have proceeded in the belief that loyalty is based, not on police restrictions, but on traditions. No doubt the security problem was made somewhat easier by the fact that Britain is an island with a largely homogeneous population; as with most islanders, the people's loyalty became entrenched through isolation.

But the years between the last two World Wars brought something new into the scene. There was a shrinkage of the "island" quality of the country through better communications from abroad. There was the influx of refugees, driven to England by the Fascist dictatorships in Europe—probably the biggest single influx of foreigners since the last invasion in 1066. And there was the spread of the international movement of Communism. Karl Marx, like Fuchs, was a German refugee in England.

These things required a new approach. But as long as the Russians were allies and the refugees and the English Communists and fellow travellers were not actively subversive—and the majority were not—security did not move against them during the war. Security then was much more concerned with watching enemy agents, the Nazis and the Fascists. The bulk of security's energies were absorbed in this from Munich on, and, in fact, no enemy agent in England of any consequence escaped during the six years of war. None operated successfully for long: they were all caught.

Then, after the war, security had to perform a *volte-face*. Counterespionage agents who had been working on Japan, Italy, and Germany were now asked to concentrate on Soviet Russia and its principal instrument, the Communist Party. There had always been surveillance of the Communists in England, of course, but it was not until 1946, or even later, that security was able to turn its full attention to them.

This was one reason why not only Fuchs but so many other Communist traitors in other countries slipped through the security net during the war. There were other specific reasons in each case, but this was the fundamental one. It is from 1946 on, when the traitors had already done their worst, that the reckoning begins.

When the Harwell Atomic Energy Establishment was set up in that same year, it was decided that in addition to its police a special security officer should also be appointed. The officer, Wing Commander Henry Arnold, arrived at Harwell a few weeks after Fuchs had come from America. In one of his earliest reports to MI 5 Arnold drew attention to the presence of Fuchs on the staff, and to the fact that he was a German who had become naturalised during the war.

A check was begun at once. It continued (without Fuchs' knowledge) for five months. There was nothing to go on beyond the report of the German Consul in Bristol—now twelve years old—which said that this distinguished and respected scientist had once in his youth been a Communist. The investigation was made simply as a precautionary measure, and it turned up nothing at all. No meeting he had, no word he uttered, and no journey he took revealed the slightest grounds for suspicion. Ironically, of course, the investigation happened to coincide with just that period, on his return from the United States, when Fuchs was dormant. It was not until just after the investigation had finished that he took up again his contacts with the Russians. This was pure bad luck; had the enquiry started a month or two later, there was every possibility that he would have been caught nearly three years earlier.

Then, in the summer of 1949, just before the explosion of the first Russian bomb, it developed from some chance evidence in the United States that, quite apart from Nunn May, the Russians had been getting information about the atomic bomb. The evidence in itself was not very precise, and it did not go very far, but the indications were that it was not an American but a British scientist who had been in touch with the Russians. This information was passed on to London by the FBI. Fuchs was not the only British scientist who had been in the United States by any means, but he did in some ways fit the case. His investigation was taken up once again.

This needed cautious handling. The information was far too slender to enable security to proceed to an arrest; the actual identity of the man himself was in doubt. There was no question of confronting Fuchs with a charge directly; if he denied it, as most certainly he would, then he would have been alerted and security would be no forwarder. There was also the possibility that he might warn his contacts and leave the country, and under

English law he could not have been stopped, since there was no direct evidence against him. Every precaution had to be taken to avoid arousing his suspicions while he was under observation. At the same time it was necessary to question him. This unexpectedly was made possible by an act of his own.

During October he came to Wing Commander Arnold and said that he wanted some advice on a personal matter that was worrying him: he had received word from Germany that his father, who was then living at Frankfort-am-Main, in the American zone, had accepted an appointment as professor of theology at the University of Leipzig, in the Russian zone. A question of security was involved. He was concerned, Fuchs said, about his own position as a senior scientist at Harwell if his father should ever get into difficulties with the Russians. Ought he to resign from Harwell? Arnold replied that he was not competent to advise Fuchs on whether he should resign—that was something for the administrative authorities. Arnold said that the question, however, was this: what *would* Fuchs do if the Russians were to put pressure on him through his father? Fuchs answered that he did not know; he might do different things in different circumstances. The two men met again a few days later, on October 20, and Fuchs repeated that he was in some doubt as to what he should do if the Russians were to arrest his father.

There were several curious aspects about this business. Doctor Fuchs had been visiting his son in England very recently. He was remembered as a lively septuagenarian, a short and active old gentleman with a ruddy face and white hair, and there had been no talk then of his going into the Russian zone. His Christian faith and his charity appeared to be remarkable (though some people thought him a garrulous old man and had doubts about his sincerity). He had brought up his dead daughter's child—the boy Fuchs was to educate in England—and he had just returned from a long stay in the United States, where he had spoken widely among the Quakers. On the other hand it also became known soon after this that his second son, Gerhardt, two years older than Klaus, was still in Switzerland, where he had had treatment at Davos for tuberculosis. Gerhardt was still a Communist.

Was it possible that the Russians were deliberately luring the old man into their zone in order to put pressure on the son? Was this blackmail to force Klaus to give information? Or was this some device of Klaus' own?

Even later on, when most of the truth came out, these points were never entirely cleared up. If the Russians had intended to blackmail Fuchs through his father, they never took occasion to do so. From the time Fuchs broke contact with them early in 1949 to the moment of his arrest he was never again approached by any agent. Nevertheless, it seems possible that Fuchs may have been deliberately trying to manoeuvre himself into a position where he could confess by drawing the attention of security to himself. Equally he might have made up his mind at this time to get out of Harwell before he was discovered, and an obvious way of doing this was to oblige the authorities to declare him a bad security risk. Both these possibilities may seem oversubtle, but they were perhaps not too subtle for the complicated state of mind in which Fuchs then found himself.

These are his own words on the matter, when he confessed later:

Shortly afterwards [after his last contact with the Russians] my father told me that he might be going into the Eastern Zone of Germany. At that time my own mind was closer to his than it had ever been before, because he also believed that they are at least trying to build a new world. He disapproved of many things and he had always done so; but he knew that when he went there he would say so, and he thought that in doing so he might help to make them realise that you cannot build a new world if you destroy some fundamental decencies in personal behaviour.

I could not bring myself to stop my father from going there. However, it made me face at least some of the facts about myself. I felt that my father's going to the Eastern Zone, that his letters, would touch me somewhere and that I was not sure whether I would not go back (presumably to Germany). I suppose I did not have the courage to fight it out for myself, and therefore I invoked an outside influence by informing security that my father was going to the Eastern Zone. A few months passed and I became more and more convinced that I had to leave Harwell.

This is the language of Othello, a man who has loved his conscience not wisely but too well, and now he is perplexed in the extreme. The crime of treason has been committed, but to no good purpose; in fact, it need never have been committed at all. And now which way to turn? Perhaps if he threw out a hint to his friend Henry Arnold, the security officer, the authorities would act and matters would be taken out of his own hands.

Yet he still clings to some vestige of logic in this mess. Sixteen years before, as a youth of 21, Fuchs had left Germany with the avowed object of getting himself educated abroad so that he could return once Hitler had been destroyed and help to rebuild a Communist fatherland. Hitler has now been destroyed, and he begins to wonder whether he should not take up that old loyalty again. Should he not go back to Germany? If his father writes to him, giving glowing accounts of affairs in the Soviet Zone, will he not be tempted? And how can he stay at Harwell in those circumstances?

Up to this point Fuchs has never had any qualms about betraying Harwell, but now he begins to develop a conscience about it. Somehow, this duality has now become intolerable; he must get rid of either Jekyll or Hyde, for he can no longer endure to live with both of them.

To Arnold and his principals, who had very little to go on, one thing at least was clear: Fuchs would have to be removed from

Harwell in some plausible manner while the investigation was going on. He could not be left with access to secret work while he was under suspicion. Already a difficulty had come up. As soon as the news of the first Russian bomb was announced it was naturally presumed at Harwell that Fuchs would be consulted about it. He was an obvious man to be asked about the size and nature of the Russian bomb. He was invited to attend one or two preliminary meetings on the matter, but it was clear that from now on he could not be told vital secrets and that the sooner he left Harwell the better.

No one envisaged that this was going to be particularly easy since by now Fuchs regarded himself as the hub of Harwell, but various proposals were considered for finding him a university post. While this matter was going forward, further information arrived from the United States which made it much more likely that Fuchs was the man they were after.

Various slight clues were beginning to appear. Sometime previously, for example, when Doctor Emil Fuchs was visiting his son at Harwell, both father and son had been invited to dinner by a colleague. Arnold had been one of the party. The dinner had passed off without incident, but now, months later, it came to Arnold's knowledge that Fuchs had been furious that Arnold had been invited. Evidently Fuchs feared that his father would blurt out something about his Communist days at Kiel University —the same fear he had expressed so long ago at Santa Fe to Harry Gold.

In the second half of December it was decided that Fuchs should be questioned outright, using as a pretext for the interrogation the fact that Fuchs himself had sought advice about his father's appointment to Leipzig. The man chosen to carry out the investigation was William James Skardon. Skardon was not a scientist, but he was one of the most able and experienced investigators in England. Since the war he had handled the cases of William Joyce and other traitors. He was a man with a quiet, self-effacing manner. It would not be difficult to imagine him as a character in one of H. G. Wells' urban stories—perhaps Mr. Kipps. He had patience and tact and considerable tenacity, and it was apparent that all these qualities were going to be needed in the handling of Klaus Fuchs before the truth came out.

On December 21 Skardon went down to Harwell, and by appointment met Fuchs in Henry Arnold's office. Outwardly the atmosphere was cordial and unexceptional—it was simply a routine meeting on a security problem between a senior Harwell executive and a security officer. After making the introduction, Arnold withdrew. Skardon opened by referring to the information Fuchs had given about his father. Was there something more that Fuchs could tell them?

For the next hour and a quarter Fuchs discussed his family background with great frankness. He confirmed that he had a sister living at 94 Lakeview Avenue, Cambridge, Massachusetts, and a brother at Davos in Switzerland. He revealed that in Kiel, in 1932, at the Social Democrat Party election for a vice-president, he had supported the Communist candidate in the absence of a Socialist. For that, Fuchs said, he was expelled from the party, and had drifted into the Communist camp. He remembered the name and address of the Quaker family who had befriended him when he first came to England in 1933; they were introduced to him through the fiancée of a cousin, and he had stayed with them at different addresses in southern England until 1937. He remembered, too, that in Bristol he had joined a committee for the defence of the Spanish democracy at the time of the Civil War.

Then there were his years with Professor Born in Edinburgh; his six months as an internee at Camp "L" and at Sherbrooke, Quebec, where he had met Hans Kahle—he had seen Kahle only once after that, at a Free German Youth Organisation meeting in London. He spoke of his work for "Tube Alloys" in Birmingham,

of his trip to the United States in 1943, and of how he had visited
his sister in Massachusetts that Christmas and again the following
spring.

All this was given by Fuchs quite calmly and readily. And then
Skardon said to him: "Were you not in touch with a Soviet official
or a Soviet representative while you were in New York? And
did you not pass on information to that person about your work?"

Fuchs opened his mouth in surprise and then smiled slightly.
"I don't think so," he said.

Skardon went on: "I am in possession of precise information
which shows that you have been guilty of espionage on behalf of
the Soviet Union; for example, during the time when you were
in New York you passed to them information concerning your
work."

When Fuchs again shook his head, saying that he did not think
so, Skardon suggested that, in view of the seriousness of the
matter, this was rather an ambiguous reply.

Fuchs answered: "I don't understand; perhaps you will tell
me what the evidence is. I have not done any such thing." He
continued then to deny any knowledge of the matter, and added
that in his opinion it had been wise to exclude Soviet Russia
from information about the atomic bomb. Skardon then went on
to other questions. Had Fuchs ever heard of Professor Halperin?
Yes; Halperin used to send him periodicals while he was interned
in Canada, but he had never met him. Fuchs remembered, however, that he (Fuchs) had made one visit to Montreal during the
time he was in New York.

At 1.30 P.M. there was a break in the interview. Fuchs went off
and lunched alone. When they resumed a little after 2 P.M.,
Skardon again confronted Fuchs with the charge of espionage,
and Fuchs again denied it, saying there was no evidence. But in
view of the suspicions about him, he said he felt he ought to
resign from Harwell. The meeting ended with another discussion

about his father's movements in Germany. The two men had been together for four hours in all, and Fuchs had shown no signs of breaking. Skardon went back to London.

Something had been gained, but not much. There had been an admission of Fuchs' activities in his youth, and there had been that inadequate phrase, "I don't think so." He had given a few details of his movements and his acquaintances. But that was all, and it was not enough. On this evidence he could not be arrested. There was always the possibility of mistaken identity.

Meanwhile, now that Fuchs had been alerted, there was the question of what next to do. If he was guilty, it was quite possible that he would try to escape from England. It was even conceivable that he would commit suicide. There were those who favoured the idea of getting him into custody on one pretext or another at once, before it was too late. But Skardon was for waiting and taking a chance; he was not yet persuaded that Fuchs was in fact the guilty man. On the other hand, he had come away from Harwell convinced that Fuchs was wrestling with a moral problem of his own. If he were given time, if he were handled carefully, there were very good hopes that in the end he would break down of his own free will. In any event, they were dependent upon getting his confession: without it they could not proceed against him. Nothing, in Skardon's opinion, should be done to antagonise Fuchs. He should be given a little more time over the Christmas holidays to think things over. Skardon did not believe that Fuchs would make any desperate move. This was not much more than a hunch—a feeling that he had established a kind of understanding with Fuchs—but in the end he had his way.

It was not until December 30, on the day after Fuchs' 38th birthday, that Skardon went down to Harwell again. He found Fuchs calm and unhurried. He again denied the charges, and said that he could not help. There was a detailed discussion of his movements in the United States in 1944, but this led to nothing new. At the end of the interview Skardon did notice that Fuchs' lips were parched, but presumably that could have happened whether Fuchs were guilty or not.

On January 10, 1950, Sir John Cockcroft sent for Fuchs and told him that in view of his father's departure for Leipzig it would be best for all concerned if Fuchs resigned from Harwell and went to some university post instead.

On January 13 Skardon came down to Harwell for a third meeting in Arnold's office. They were again left alone. Did Fuchs remember the exact address of his apartment in New York in 1944? Nearly six years had gone by, and he was not quite certain of it. However, with the aid of a map he identified the place as West 77th Street, near Central Park, in the middle of a block between Columbus Avenue and Amsterdam Avenue. When Skardon told him that security was pressing enquiries about this apartment and other matters in New York, Fuchs appeared unconcerned. He still denied all the charges. He said he knew now, however, that he would have to leave Harwell. It should not be difficult, he said, for him to find a university post. But first he would take a holiday.

This, then, was the impasse reached after three long meetings. All along Skardon had urged upon Fuchs that security was not trying to ruin him. If some slip had been made in New York during the war, then it was much better to have the thing out in the open. Fuchs was a valuable man at Harwell. It was always possible that once this business was thrashed out some arrangement could be made to enable him to continue with his work. But the present strain was intolerable for everybody.

Fuchs himself was very well aware that as yet security had no inkling of the real extent of his treason, nor of its long duration. Through this fortnight in January, then, he was asking himself: "Shall I admit the lesser crime if they will let me stay on at Harwell? But then, even if I remain at Harwell, can I trust myself not to turn traitor again?"

He revealed all this in his confession when he said:

I was then confronted with the fact that there was evidence that I had given away information in New York. I was given the chance of admitting it and staying at Harwell or clearing out. I was not sure enough of myself to stay at Harwell, and therefore I denied the allegation and decided that I would have to leave Harwell.

However, it became clear to me that in leaving Harwell in these circumstances I would do two things. I would deal a grave blow to Harwell, to all the work which I have loved; and furthermore that I would leave suspicions against people whom I had loved, who were my friends and who believed that I was their friend.

I had to face the fact that it had been possible for me in one half of my mind to be friends with people, to be close friends, and at the same time to deceive them and to endanger them. I had to realise that the control mechanism had warned me of danger to myself, but that it had also prevented me from realising what I was doing to people close to me.

I then realised that the combination of the three ideas which had made me what I was, was wrong: in fact every single one of them was wrong: that there are certain standards of moral behaviour which are in you and that you cannot disregard. That in your actions you must be clear in your own mind whether they are right or wrong. That you must be able, before accepting somebody else's authority, to state your doubts and try and resolve them. And I found that at least I myself was made by circumstances.

This is very complicated. But several clear things come out of it. He is not quite humble yet; he regards himself as quite essential to Harwell, and by leaving he perceived he would deal it a grave blow. But now at last he is aware of the feelings of his friends. They will be hurt. Suspicion might fall on them. He had never thought of this before because the "control mechanism" had prevented him from taking account of anything as minor as the human beings around him whom he had betrayed. They were the casual victims of his grand design for the perfection of the world.

But now he realised he had no right to hurt them. This was a considerable advance but Fuchs was still a long way off from realising the real enormity of what he had done; he still could not see that what mattered was not his friends' feelings, but the fact that they and everybody else on this earth might be blown to smithereens as a consequence of his treason. This point never seems to have entered his mind, then or since. He was obsessed throughout by his own personal moral position.

After the January 13 meeting, Skardon was on slightly firmer ground. Nothing definite had happened, but an atmosphere of confidence had been created, and he felt sure that Fuchs would make no move without consulting him. The two men, the hunter and the quarry, were entering now into that strange, intensely intimate world of criminal investigation where personal animosities cease to count any more, and where each man trusts the other, even though they know that before the end one of them has got to be destroyed. There is an insect quality about this business— the slow, inevitable waiting of the spider for the fly. The fly has to be caught, and the spider has to pounce, and there is nothing either of them can do about it.

Fuchs was not quite ready yet. Outwardly he remained perfectly calm. He went about his work in the normal way, and he confided in nobody. His friends at Harwell knew nothing of what was going on, and they noticed nothing peculiar about him. There was just one incident.

A scandal broke out among the members of Fuchs' own staff. It was nothing more than an untidy love affair gone wrong, an incident of the kind that happens in every garrison, but which at the time seems outrageous because of the special intimacy of garrison life. This matter affected Fuchs to some extent—he made a point of visiting the distracted woman in hospital—and it might have been that he felt that this was one more sign that the life at Harwell he knew and liked so well was breaking up around him.

At all events, the incident seems to have brought him to a decision at last. On Sunday, January 22, Fuchs phoned Arnold and said he wanted a private talk. They arranged to lunch at the old Railway House Hotel at Steventon on the following day. At that luncheon there was some discussion of politics—Fuchs said he was opposed to Communism as practised in Russia now—and he also said he should like to see Skardon again; he had something more to tell him. It was agreed that the meeting should take place at Fuchs' "prefab" at 11 A.M. next day, Tuesday, January 24.

Arnold met Skardon at Didcot railway station and drove him to Harwell. Skardon walked down to "prefab" No. 17 alone. It was ten days or more since the two men had met, and the change in Fuchs was remarkable. He looked unusually pale, and he seemed to Skardon to be in a state of some agitation. When Skardon said, "You asked to see me, and here I am," Fuchs answered at once, "Yes. It's rather up to me now."

But having made that half admission he stopped—as though overtaken by some sudden misgiving about what he had to say. While Skardon waited he went wandering off into a long dissertation about his life, going over and over again the details they had discussed so much before—his underground days in Berlin, his father (who by now had left for Leipzig), his friends at Harwell, the importance of his work at Harwell, the need for him at Harwell. He told the story of his career again, giving nothing new, but talking with his head in his hands and his face haggard.

After two hours of this, Skardon said: "You have told me a long story providing the motives for actions, but nothing about the actions themselves."

Why couldn't Klaus break down? Why not confess and have done with it? He was only torturing himself. If only he would give way, then Skardon might be able to help him.

Fuchs paused, and then answered steadily: "I will never be persuaded by you to talk."

"All right," Skardon said, "let's have some lunch."

There was a luncheon van that went round the Harwell compound selling fish and chips and other snacks. Skardon indicated this van, which was passing the house just then, and said, "Will we have some fish and chips?"

Fuchs answered, "No. Let's go into Abingdon."

They got into Fuchs' grey saloon car, with Fuchs at the wheel, and on the five-mile run into Abingdon he drove with a reckless, breakneck speed that bordered on insanity. He cut corners on the wrong side of the road, he passed all other traffic with inches to spare; and they raced at last through the streets of Abingdon up to the door of the principal hotel.

An English pub on a wet winter's afternoon is not a place that lends itself easily to high drama. There were other guests in the dining room. Skardon and Fuchs ate their way through a prosaic meal, talking about the gossip of Harwell, about the different personalities there, about anything but treason. It was a strained and desultory conversation.

Then they went into the lounge for coffee. Skardon spoke of Professor Skinner's departure from Harwell and asked who was going to take his place. Fuchs said he did not know.

"You are number three, aren't you?" Skardon said. "Might you not have got the job?"

"Possibly," Fuchs said, and Skardon slightly shook his head. There was no likelihood of that now—not at any rate until Fuchs had confessed. Suddenly Fuchs jumped up and said, "Let's go back."

They returned to Harwell with excruciating slowness. For a great part of the way they drove behind a lorry travelling at barely ten miles an hour, and Fuchs would not pass it. They got out in silence at the "prefab," and as soon as they were inside Fuchs made his announcement. He had decided to confess, he said. His conscience was clear, but he was worried about his friends in Harwell and what they might think.

"When did it start?" Skardon asked.

"About the middle of 1942," Fuchs answered, "and it had continued until about a year ago."

That was seven years. That covered the whole period of the bomb, its conception, its construction, and its explosion. It covered the years in England, as well as those in New York and Los Alamos. This was the first shock Skardon had that afternoon. It was the first intimation that he or anybody else had had that they were dealing here, not with the leakage of a few facts and figures, but with treason on an immense scale and for a very long time.

And now that he had started, now that he was beginning to feel the relief of confession, Fuchs ran on quickly, recounting unbelievable facts. There had been frequent but irregular meetings, he said. He had taken the initiative. He had spoken to an intermediary who had arranged the first interview, and after that, through all these seven years, each meeting had been arranged in advance with an alternative.

At first Fuchs had told the Russians merely the products of his own brain, but as time went on this had developed into something more, until he had given them everything he knew. His contacts were sometimes Russians, sometimes people of other nationalities. He realised that he was carrying his life in his hands, but he had learned to do that in his underground days in Germany. He went on to speak of his meetings in New York, at Los Alamos, and more recently in London, until he failed to go to his February rendezvous in 1949, and the Russians had not approached him since. All the meetings were short: he handed over documents, fixed the next rendezvous, and then departed. Sometimes his contact asked him questions, but these questions were not the questions of the contact, but of someone else with technical knowledge.

All this came out in a rapid voice, and it was no moment for

Skardon to take notes or to interrupt. As soon as he could, he
asked: what had Fuchs actually given the Russians?—and he
received then his second shock that afternoon.

He supposed, Fuchs said, that the worst thing he had done was
to tell the Russians the method of making the atomic bomb.

Now finally the truth was out, and it could not have been worse.
Any possibility of Fuchs remaining at Harwell or anywhere else
except inside a prison was obviously out of the question. All that
could be done now was to extract from him every last damning
fact, and so manage him that he would continue to talk until he
had nothing left to say. Now that the break had come, and he was
sure that Fuchs was pinned at last, Skardon was only anxious to
end the interview as soon as possible so that he could take advice
and get the full confession down in writing.

But Fuchs wanted to go on. He explained carefully that it
was impossible for him, of course, to do more than tell the
Russians the principle on which the bomb was made. It was up
to the Russians to produce their own industrial equipment, and
he had been astonished when they had succeeded in making and
detonating a bomb as soon as the previous August. He knew,
Fuchs said, that scientifically they were sufficiently advanced,
but he had not supposed that commercially and industrially they
were so far developed.

As for his own information, he had been gradually diminishing
it over the past two years. That was because he began to have
doubts about what he was doing. He still believed in Communism, he said, but not as now practised by Russia—that sort
of Communism was something to fight against. He had decided
that the only place for him to live was in England, and he returned again to the subject of his friends. What were they going
to think about his behaviour—especially Henry Arnold, whom he
had deceived most of all?

He insisted that his sister Kristel in the United States knew

nothing of his contact with the Russians; if she had noticed anything suspicious she would have thought it was part of his
underground activities on behalf of the German Communist
Party.

He added one or two more scraps of information before
Skardon brought the interview to an end. A typical place of
rendezvous in London was Mornington Crescent. He was never
given an alias by the Russians—they knew him simply as Fuchs,
and he could not remember what all the various signals of recognition were. Just once he had taken a gift of £100, as a symbol of
his subservience to the cause.

Fuchs was now much calmer and more self-possessed. He
agreed that, since they were both tired, it would be best to break
off and meet another time. The afternoon meeting had lasted just
an hour. When should they meet again? Skardon asked. Fuchs
recalled that he had a committee meeting the following day, so
that would not be a suitable time. But the day after that, January
26, he would be free.

On this, Skardon left Fuchs at his doorway and drove back to
London with possibly the most sinister report any man has ever
had to deliver. What gave the affair a special sense of unreality
was that Fuchs, having unburdened himself, still believed that
all would be well—they would still continue to employ him at
Harwell. Indeed, in the course of the interview he had made it
clear that this was the reason why he had invited Skardon to
Harwell and had confessed. He had been a Russian agent. That
was a mistake, and now he had admitted it. But he had ceased to
be a Russian agent. Now it was up to Skardon to explain all this
to the authorities and wind up any tiresome official formalities as
quickly as possible so that Fuchs could get on with his work. He
had resolved not to take a university post outside Harwell; it
was no longer necessary. He had confessed, and that was that. It
was all over and done with. And the price Skardon had to pay for

the confession was that he had to ensure that Fuchs remained on at Harwell.

Fuchs, in other words, was still a thousand miles away from any understanding of the real issues at stake. Yet there were certain advantages for security in his absurd illusions. So long as he was thinking along these lines it was not likely that he would bolt, nor would he commit suicide. Moreover, he would help in every way he could. More than ever now, it was necessary not to alarm him, not to surround him with police, not to drag him down from the dream world in which he was still living.

The next meeting, on January 26, again took place at Harwell. Fuchs seemed to have maintained his composure during the intervening two days, and he was ready with a mass of details about his meetings with his contacts in London, Boston, New York, and Santa Fe. He had been to see Arnold in the interval, and at that painful meeting it was one more unreality to be added to all the rest that Fuchs should have said he was a little worried lest Skardon had not appreciated the significance and importance of the whole affair. In particular he was concerned about the forthcoming declassification meeting with the Americans at which Fuchs was to be one of the British representatives. Did Skardon appreciate that it was absolutely essential for Fuchs to be there? If he were not people would notice his absence. Suspicions would be aroused. And this would be a very bad thing for Harwell. Did Skardon understand that? Arnold had reassured Fuchs, and suggested he might raise the matter at his next meeting with Skardon.

And now, on January 26, Fuchs urged Skardon to move in the matter as quickly as possible, as he was anxious to have his position clarified.

Skardon put forward three choices: either Fuchs could write out a confession himself, he could dictate it to a secretary, or he could dictate it to Skardon himself. Fuchs at once chose the last course, and it was arranged that they should meet the following day in a room at the War Office in London. The understanding between the two men was now complete. The fly was in the web, but he was held there by nothing visible. They were on a Christian name basis, they had a certain respect for one another, and to Fuchs at least it seemed that they were acting out their parts merely as instruments of some sort of inevitable fate that was larger than themselves. After the drama was over they could go away and take up their normal lives again.

Certainly after nearly eight years of silence, of living the double life and never confiding in anybody, it must have been an immense relief for Fuchs at last to telescope his two lives into one, and for the first time tell the story—the whole story—to someone who would sympathise and understand. That was the important thing—to be understood. To make oneself perfectly and precisely clear. As soon as Skardon had left Fuchs had a talk with Arnold, and very readily answered questions on what kind of information he had passed on to the Russians.

The following day, January 27, still in this mood of confession, Fuchs came up to London without police supervision of any kind. Skardon met him at Paddington Station and drove him to the War Office in Whitehall. They sat down, and when Skardon gave him the usual official caution, and asked him if he were ready to make a statement, Fuchs answered, "Yes, I quite understand. I would like you to carry on."

Skardon took the confession down by hand.

I am deputy Chief Scientific Officer (acting rank) at Atomic Energy Research Establishment, Harwell [it began]. I was born in Russelsheim on December 29, 1911. My father was a parson and I had a very happy childhood. I think that the one thing that stands out is that my father always did what he believed to be the right thing to do, and he always told us that we had to go our own way even if he disagreed. He himself had many fights because he did what his conscience decreed, even if this meant that he was at variance with accepted conventions. For example, he was the first parson to join the social democratic party.

So it went on through the whole involved story. It was when they were drawing to the end of it that Fuchs for the first time had something to say of his contrition.

I know that I cannot go back on that [on what had happened] and I know that all I can do now is to try and repair the damage I have done. The first thing is to make sure that Harwell will suffer as little as possible and that I have to save for my friends as much as possible of that part that was good in my relations with them. This thought is at present uppermost in my mind, and I find it difficult to concentrate on any other points.

However, I realise that I will have to state the extent of the information I have given and that I shall have to help as far as my conscience allows me in stopping other people who are still doing what I have done. There is nobody I know by name who is concerned with collecting information for the Russian authorities. There are people whom I know by sight whom I trusted with my life and who trusted me with theirs, and I do not know that I shall be able to do anything that might in the end give them away. They are not inside the project, but they are intermediaries between myself and the Russian Government.

At first I thought that all I would do would be to inform the Russian authorities that work on the atomic bomb was going on. I concentrated at first mainly on the product of my own work, but in particular at Los Alamos I did what I consider to be the worst I have done, namely to give information about the principle of the design of the plutonium bomb.

Later on at Harwell I began to be concerned about the information I was giving, and I began to sift it, but it is difficult to say exactly when and how I did it because it was a process which went up and down with my inner struggles. The last time when I handed over information was in February or March 1949.

Before I joined the project most of the English people with whom I made personal contacts were left wing, and affected in some degree or other by the same kind of philosophy. Since coming to Harwell I have met English people of all kinds, and I have come to see in many of them a deep-rooted firmness which enables them to lead a decent way of life. I do not know where this springs from and I don't think they do, but it is there.

I have read this statement and to the best of my knowledge it is true.

He signed then "Klaus Fuchs," and Skardon made a note at the bottom that Fuchs had read the statement through, made such alterations as he wished, and had initialled each and every page.

Fuchs had one more reservation, however, and that in itself was part of the moral wonderland in which he was still firmly drifting: he would not tell Skardon the technical details of the construction of the atomic bomb that he had passed on to the Russians, because Skardon had not been cleared for access to such information. He agreed to confide in a qualified person, Mr. Michael Perrin, whom he had known since 1942 as the assistant to Sir Wallace Akers at "Tube Alloys," and who had stayed on with the Atomic Energy Division in the Ministry of Supply. An appointment was fixed for January 30 in London; Fuchs said he would like a rest over the weekend to gather his thoughts. He again repeated that he was anxious about his future, and did not want to waste time in getting it settled. He then returned alone to Harwell by train.

That same night a strange thing happened. Arnold got word that there was a light burning in Fuchs' office. He went at once to the administrative block and quietly let himself in. A light was indeed burning in Fuchs' room, and there were sounds that indicated that there was someone inside.

Arnold used his pass key to get into a room which was directly opposite across a corridor. The partitions between these offices in the administrative block have glass panes let into them about eight feet from the floor, close to the ceiling. By getting up on a cupboard Arnold found he could look across the corridor into Fuchs' room. Fuchs was sitting there at his desk, going through his papers. His cabinet was open, and as he read he smoked. The rest of the building was in darkness and silence.

For a long time Arnold watched him. At that moment many things were still possible. It could still have been that Fuchs was intending to commit suicide after all. He might also have been planning to escape from England in the night, taking his papers with him. Again, he might merely have come here to destroy those papers.

Arnold watched and waited. But Fuchs continued quietly reading, pausing occasionally to take other documents from the cabinet and sort them out in piles on the desk. Then, toward 11 o'clock, he got up, left his papers on the desk and the light burning, locked the door behind him, and went out. Arnold calculated that Fuchs was bound to come back, if only to put out the light, and he remained standing on the cupboard in the darkness.

It was an hour, however, and close to midnight, before Fuchs returned. Then he sat down and began reading again as he had before. This continued for another half-hour or more, while still Arnold watched and waited. Then at last, about 12.30 A.M., Fuchs got up, locked his office door, put out the light, got into his car, and drove home. Arnold then entered the room and found that the papers which Fuchs had been reading dealt only with routine matters and were not important. The room, with the papers still spread out on the desk, remained untouched until it was officially searched after Fuchs' arrest.

Fuchs took a morning train up to London on Monday, January 30. He arrived at Paddington at 10.45 A.M., and Skardon brought him to the War Office, where Perrin was waiting. As they went into the meeting Fuchs said he had remembered one or two

other facts about his contacts that might be useful. He said he was
certain that there were other scientists besides himself who had
been working for the Russians. Also he recalled now the place of
the last rendezvous which he had failed to attend. It was the
Spotted Dog at Putney, or alternatively another pub near Wood
Green underground station.

Skardon opened the proceedings with Perrin by saying that
Fuchs had decided to reveal everything. Perrin replied that he
had plenty of notepaper, and they set to work. They went
through the seven years of meetings chronologically, noting just
what Fuchs had given to the Russians at each time and place:
at first, his monthly reports when he was working with "Tube
Alloys" in Birmingham in 1942; then, in New York, the details
of the gaseous diffusion process; then, at Santa Fe, the principles
of the plutonium bomb; and finally, at Harwell, the information
about the progress of the postwar British project.

It was a long business and after an hour or two the three men
broke off for lunch. They went to a hotel behind the War Office
in Whitehall, close to Scotland Yard, and finding all the tables
occupied, perched themselves at the snack bar, as strange a
luncheon party as any in London that day. Then they went
back to work again.

Fuchs repeated to Perrin that he was convinced that other
scientists were at work for the Russians and had been all along.
As an example, he described how, very early in his espionage,
while he was still in England, they had asked him for details
of the electromagnetic isotope separation process in Berkeley,
California, and that was a matter of which no British scientist
had any knowledge at that time.

It was 4 P.M. when the statement was finished. Fuchs then
went off alone to Harwell, while Perrin got his notes typed;
it was a long document of many pages. Now at last the authorities had enough. There were still a number of details to be got

from Fuchs, but now they knew the worst. It was time to make the arrest.

There was an election going on in England at the time—the election that brought Labour back with a small majority in 1950 —and the legal formalities were complicated. First, the Prime Minister, Mr. Attlee, had to be acquainted with the confession. Then the Attorney General, Sir Hartley Shawcross, had to be found—he was somewhere in the north of England. Shawcross returned to London, reading through the case in the train, and in London the Special Branch at Scotland Yard and others worked on the precise wording of the charge. These matters occupied the whole of January 31 and February 1. By February 2 they were ready to move.

Security preferred not to make the arrest inside Harwell, where nothing was yet known of the investigation. Instead, they decided to get Fuchs quietly to London, and the best way of doing this was for Perrin to telephone Fuchs and ask him to come up for a further interview. The arrest would take place at Perrin's office at Shell-Mex House. Perrin agreed to do this—though as a layman he lacked some of security's enthusiasm for the idea. His only stipulation was that if Fuchs was going to be arrested in his office, he, Perrin, should not be present. He got through to Fuchs by phone on the morning of February 2, and said: "Can you come up again this afternoon?" Fuchs agreed, and suggested a train from Didcot which would get into Paddington around 2.30 P.M.; it was a journey of little more than an hour.

It was arranged then that Commander Leonard Burt of Scotland Yard should be present in Perrin's room at 2.30 P.M., with the charge and a warrant for Fuchs' arrest. Perrin, somewhat restlessly, took up position in his office at 2.30; and then for half an hour nothing whatever happened. Perrin telephoned security, and was assured that Burt was on his way. At 3 o'clock Perrin's secretary telephoned through to say that Fuchs had arrived. Perrin gave instructions that Fuchs should be kept in his outer office until Burt appeared, and in some agitation he telephoned security once again.

Finally, at 3.20 P.M., Burt arrived with a police inspector, and they were shown at once into Perrin's room. The delay had been caused by last-minute arrangements over the wording of the charge. They then sent for Fuchs, who had been waiting all this time in the adjoining room. Perrin introduced him quickly to Burt, and then slipped away into another room. Burt read out the charge at once and told Fuchs he was under arrest. Fuchs made no comment. He sat down in Perrin's chair, and then asked if he could see Perrin himself.

Burt agreed and brought Perrin back into the room again. Fuchs' face had suddenly gone grey. Now at last the whole elaborate dream edifice had collapsed, and looking directly at Perrin, he made his final absurd and touching *cri de coeur:* "You realise what this will mean at Harwell?"

The officers noted that down and took him away to Bow Street Police Station.

Eleven

•

FUCHS' THREE APPEARANCES IN COURT ARE REMARKABLE FOR THEIR brevity, for what was not said or given in evidence, and for the dispatch with which they were managed. He was never allowed bail, and within a month of his arrest he had been arraigned, tried, and sentenced. He himself spoke only once or twice, and very briefly, and he uttered nothing in his own defence.

His first appearance was before the Chief Magistrate, Sir Laurence Dunne, at Bow Street, on February 3, the day following his arrest, and this was a purely formal proceeding. Commander Burt, the only witness, related the circumstances under which the arrest had been made. Fuchs said he had no questions to ask of Burt, and the magistrate said to him: "Is there anything you want me to do for you in the way of legal representation?" Fuchs answered, "I don't know of anybody." The magistrate asked if he was a man of means, and the prosecutor, Mr. Christmas Humphreys, replied, "Yes, there is no reason to think he cannot afford to pay for legal representation. He has a substantial salary." The magistrate ordered that the prisoner's spectacles and other articles which were taken from him at the time of his arrest should be returned to him, and the case was then remanded for a week while Fuchs obtained lawyers and the prosecution prepared their brief. Fuchs remained at Brixton Prison.

At the second hearing at Bow Street on February 10, Wing Commander Arnold, Skardon, and Perrin all gave evidence, but the confession was not given in court. The prosecutor, Mr. Humpheys, said this:

> The mind of Fuchs may possibly be unique, and create a new precedent in the world of psychology. It is clear from his statement that he had half of his mind beyond the reach of reason and the impact of facts. The other half lived in a world of normal relationships and friendship with his colleagues and human loyalty. This dual personality has been consciously and deliberately produced. He broke his mind in two, describing it as controlled schizophrenia. He has produced in himself a classic example of the immortal duality in English literature, Jekyll and Hyde.

Fuchs again had nothing to say and he was committed for trial at the Old Bailey.

Three weeks then went by while Fuchs was held at Brixton Prison, and then, on March 1, he appeared before the Lord Chief Justice, Lord Goddard, in the same court in which Allan Nunn May had been tried and sentenced four years before. The case had now attracted very wide attention in the newspapers. They recorded the appearance of the Lord Chief Justice, with his scarlet and ermine, coming into court behind the sword-bearer and the mace-bearer in their mediaeval costumes, and the hush in the crowded court as he settled into his chair under the sword of justice. They recorded the presence of the Duchess of Kent, and a number of other notable people in court, and that a Miss Giesler Wagner, a cousin of the prisoner and his only relative in England, was there too. They noted that Fuchs was attended by a doctor, that he looked pale, that throughout the hearing his eyes remained fixed on the bench, and that he made no sign of any kind.

But there was no great drama in court that day—nothing as
sensational as the extraordinary nature of the problem itself. The
case was over in an hour and a half, and Skardon was the only
witness. Yet those ninety minutes must have been for Fuchs
one of the strangest anticlimaxes any man has ever experienced
for he had just heard, as he came into the court, that he was not
going to die. His senior counsel, Mr. Derek Curtis-Bennett, had
seen him in the cells immediately before the hearing began
and had told him that there was not much hope. Counsel would
do their best, but there was no chance of an acquittal, and he
had to expect the maximum penalty. Fuchs had answered, "Yes.
I understand."

"You know what the maximum penalty is?" Curtis-Bennett
asked, and Fuchs replied, "Yes, I know. It's death." He had apparently believed all this time he had been in prison that he was
about to die.

"No," said Curtis-Bennett. "No. It is fourteen years."

Upon this Fuchs made no sign of relief or surprise; he went
on calmly into court, followed the proceedings closely, and spoke
up clearly and firmly at the end.

He was charged with having communicated to unknown persons information which might be useful to an enemy, on four
separate occasions: in Birmingham, in 1943; in New York, between December 1943 and August 1944; in Boston, in February
1945; and in Berkshire, England, in 1947. Fuchs pleaded guilty
to all four counts.

The Attorney General, Sir Hartley Shawcross, opened for the
Crown.

The prisoner [he said] is a Communist, and that is at once the
explanation and indeed the tragedy of this case. Quite apart from
the great harm the prisoner has done the country that he adopted
and which adopted him, it is a tragedy that one of such high intellectual attainments as the prisoner possesses, should have allowed his

mental processes to have become so warped by his devotion to communism that, as he himself expresses it, he became a kind of controlled schizophrenic, the dominant half of his mind leading him to do things which the other part of his mind recognised quite clearly were wrong. Indeed, my Lord, his statement (and so far as we have been able to check it, we believe his statement to be true) is a very object lesson in the meaning of communism, and before I say a word as to the facts, perhaps I might be permitted to add this, because it has an immediate bearing on the case:

In this country the number of Communists is fortunately very few, and it may be that a great number of those people who support the Communist movement believe, as the prisoner at one time apparently believed, misguidedly if sincerely, that that movement is seeking to build a new world. What they don't realise is that it is to be a world dominated by a single power, and that the supporters of the Communist Party, the true adherents of communism, indoctrinated with the Communist belief, must become traitors to their own country, in the interests—or what they are told are the interests—of the international Communist movement.

My Lord, it was because of these facts that this brilliant scientist, as he is, now undoubtedly disillusioned and ashamed, came to place his country and himself in this terrible position.

Sir Hartley then gave an account of Fuchs' career, quoting largely from the confession. He made the point that the confession was not obtained by any sinister pressure, nor after any "long period of secret incarceration incommunicado." Skardon supported this in the witness box, and added that since his arrest Fuchs had done all he could to help the authorities.

Curtis-Bennett at the outset based his case on the intense political pressure which had been put upon Fuchs in his youth in Germany. He said:

Then the struggle burst into flames in February 1933, when somebody set the Reichstag on fire, which was the next door house of the President of the Reichstag. There was a screech throughout Germany against the Communists. This scientist, this scholarly man, read that news in the newspaper on the train the morning after it happened. He went underground, scarcely saving his own life, and came to this country in 1933 for the purpose of conducting his scientific studies in order to fit himself out to be a scientist to help in the rebuilding of a Communist Germany, not to throw atom bombs at anybody, but to study physics.

A theoretical physicist, he was educated at Kiel University, Leipzig University, Bristol University, and Edinburgh University. He pursued his peaceful studies, and had not the War come he might have been a candidate for a Nobel Peace Prize or a membership of the Royal Society rather than for gaol.

"In England," said Mr. Curtis-Bennett, "Fuchs never pretended to be anything but a Communist."

Lord Goddard: "I don't know whether you are suggesting that was known to the authorities."

Curtis-Bennett: "I don't know—but he made no secret of the fact."

Lord Goddard: "I don't suppose he proclaimed himself as a Communist when naturalised or when taken into Harwell or when he went to the U.S.A."

Curtis-Bennett: "If I am wrong Mr. Attorney General will correct me. It was on his records in this country at the Home Office that he was a member of the German Communist Party."

Sir Hartley Shawcross: "It was realised when he was examined by the Enemy Aliens Tribunal at the beginning of the war that he was a refugee from Nazi persecution, because in Germany he had been a Communist. All the investigations at that time and since have not shown that he had any association whatever with British members of the Communist Party."

All he wished to say, Curtis-Bennett went on, was this: ". . . anybody who has read anything of Marxist theory must

know that any man who is a Communist, whether in Germany
or Timbuctoo, will react in exactly the same way when he comes
into possession of information. He will almost automatically, un-
happily, put his allegiance to the Communist ideology first. . . .
He had a sort of sieve in his mind about the information he
would or would not give, and in Count One, 1943——"

Lord Goddard: "I have read this statement with very great care
more than once. I cannot understand this metaphysical philosophy, or whatever you like to call it. I am not concerned with
it. I am concerned that this man gave away secrets of vital importance to this country. He stands before me as a sane man, and
not relying on the disease of schizophrenia or anything else."

Curtis-Bennett: "If Your Lordship does not think that the state
of mind a man acts under is relative to sentence——"

Lord Goddard: "A man in that state of mind is one of the
most dangerous that this country could have within its shores."

Curtis-Bennett: "I have to endeavour to put before Your Lordship this man as he is, knowing that Your Lordship is not
going to visit him savagely, but justly, both in the interests of the
state and the interests of this man, and I can only try to explain
what Your Lordship has said you fail to understand. Though I
fail in the end, I can do no more, but do it I must. There was
acting in his mind a sieve whereby, with regard to the first count,
he would only tell things he found out himself. He is a scientist,
a pencil-and-paper man, and it is good to hear the Attorney say
that it is not in his power to make an atom bomb and hand it
over to the Russians—to give away a mighty secret of that sort.
In 1943 he gave information about what he himself knew out of
his own head. I am not going to confuse this case with long
medical terms. He is not mad. He is sane. But he is a human
being, and that is what I am trying to explain."

Curtis-Bennett explained how the sieve of Fuchs' mind got
wider until he gave the Russians all he knew, and then finally,

on his return to England, the sieve closed up. He first gave the information because Russia was an ally, and after the war it was only logical for him to continue to do so.

"A scientist," Curtis-Bennett continued, "is in this position: he is taught, or teaches himself, or learns, that A plus B equals C. If he is told tomorrow that it is A minus B that equals C, he does not believe it. But your sensible citizen or politician, moving in the affairs of the world, told that, would agree with both. He has to. But the change of political alignments is not the business of scientists, for scientists are not always politically wise. Their minds move along straight lines, without the flexibility that some others have."

Finally, Curtis-Bennett said, Fuchs had recanted. "There you have this man being logical, in my submission: having decided to tell everything, tells everything, makes it about as bad for himself as he can, and provides the whole of the case against him in this court. There is not one piece of evidence produced in the case which is not the result of the written and oral statements he made to Mr. Skardon in December and January of this year."

No further evidence was produced. Lord Goddard told Fuchs he was convicted, and asked him if he had anything to say. Fuchs then gave the only public statement he had made since his arrest. He said:

My Lord, I have committed certain crimes, for which I am charged, and I expect sentence. I have also committed some other crimes, which are not crimes in the eyes of the law—crimes against my friends; and when I asked my counsel to put certain facts before you, I did not do it because I wanted to lighten my sentence. I did it in order to atone for those other crimes.

I have had a fair trial, and I wish to thank you and my counsel and my solicitors. I also wish to thank the Governor and his staff of Brixton Prison for the considerate treatment they have given me.

This was Lord Goddard's summing up:

In 1933, fleeing from political persecution in Germany, you took advantage of the right of asylum, or the privilege of asylum, which has always been the boast of this country to people persecuted in their own country for their political opinions. You betrayed the hospitality and protection given you by the grossest treachery.

In 1942, in return for your offer to put at the service of this country the great gifts Providence has bestowed upon you in scientific matters, you were granted British nationality. From that moment, regardless of your oath, you started to betray secrets of vital importance for the purpose of furthering a political creed held in abhorrence by the vast majority in this country, your object being to strengthen that creed which was then known to be inimical to all freedom-loving countries.

There are four matters which seem to me to be the gravest aspects of your crime. In the first, by your conduct you have imperilled the right of asylum which this country has hitherto extended. Dare we now give shelter to political refugees who may be followers of this pernicious creed, and disguise themselves and then treacherously bite the hand that feeds them?

Secondly, you have betrayed not only the projects and inventions of your own brain for which this country was paying you and enabling you to live in comfort in return for your promises of secrecy. You have also betrayed the secrets of other workers in this field of science, not only in this country, but in the United States, and thereby you might have caused the gravest suspicions to fall on those you falsely treated as friends and who were misled into trusting you.

Thirdly, you might have imperiled the good relations between this country and the great American republic with which His Majesty is aligned.

And fourthly, you have done irreparable and incalculable harm both to this land and to the United States, and you did it, as your statement shows, merely for the purpose of furthering your political creed, for I am willing to assume you have not done it for gain.

Your statement, which has been read, shows to me the depth of self-deception into which people like yourself can fall. Your crime to me is only thinly differentiated from high treason. In this country we observe rigidly the rule of law, and as technically it is not high treason, so you are not tried for that offence. *

I have now to assess the penalty which it is right I should impose. It is not so much for punishment that I impose it, for punishment can mean nothing to a man of your mentality.

My duty is to safeguard this country; and how can I be sure that a man, whose mentality is shown in that statement you have made, may not, at any other minute, allow some curious working of your mind to lead you further to betray secrets of the greatest possible value and importance to this land?

The maximum sentence which Parliament has ordained for this crime is fourteen years' imprisonment, and that is the sentence I pass upon you.

Without any further word, or any visible display of emotion, Fuchs left the dock.

This time no one came forward to protest against the sentence, as they had done in the case of Allan Nunn May. Instead, there was a very sober feeling that something had happened here which was beyond the power of any court to punish or correct. It was not just a question of the prisoner Fuchs, or the intriguing duality of the Communist mind. The whole question of British security was involved. How far had security slipped? How many other Fuchses were running around in the British and American laboratories? How was it possible that a traitor could walk through all the security barriers in England and America, and for years, without anyone being the wiser?

Several events followed rapidly. On March 3, 1950, the Prime Minister, Mr. Attlee, saw Sir Percy Sillitoe, the head of MI 5, in Downing Street, and the documents in the case were sent to Mr. Truman and the FBI in the United States. Mr. Truman had

* In England the charge of high treason, for which the penalty is death, can be made only against a traitor who assists an enemy. Fuchs gave information to an ally.

already announced in February that the United States would press on with the manufacture of the hydrogen bomb. But this was to be purely an American effort; the exchange of atomic weapons information with Britain had already ceased since the war.

On March 6 Mr. Attlee made a statement on Fuchs to the House of Commons. This we can more conveniently deal with later.

On March 7 the Tass Agency published a statement that the Soviet Government had no knowledge of Fuchs and that no agent of theirs had been in contact with him—a claim so blatantly and childishly false that one wonders why they ever bothered to make it. On March 10 the Joint Congressional Committee on Atomic Energy met in Washington, and it had before it the two vital documents—the first confession to Skardon and the second—technical—confession to Perrin. The committee was, in the word of its chairman, Senator MacMahon, "shocked." A hunt to track down Fuchs' contacts was begun on both sides of the Atlantic.

Fuchs in prison was repeatedly questioned and shown hundreds of photographs. He had known none of his contacts by their real names, and in the intervening years he had forgotten very largely what they looked like. He actually passed over a photograph of Harry Gold, saying he had never seen him before. The FBI concentrated on Gold. They sent two men, Hugh Clegg and Robert Lamphere, to question Fuchs in England, they made minute enquiries of hundreds of possible suspects in the United States, they questioned Fuchs' sister Kristel; and finally, on May 22, when they were convinced that Gold must be their man, they got him to confess. It was the map of Santa Fe which Gold had bought so that he could find his way to his rendezvous with Fuchs in 1945 that was his undoing. When the FBI searched his apartment and discovered this map, Gold was so utterly taken aback that he broke down. And it happened that within an hour of his arrest word came from England that Fuchs had at last identified Gold from some motion pictures of him which had been taken a short time before.

From Gold the trail then led to David Greenglass, to the Rosenbergs, and to others in the American spy ring. In England, where a similar hunt was in progress, it was found that most of Fuchs' contacts had already decamped to Soviet Germany. About this time also, Fuchs' elder brother, Gerhardt, was expelled from Switzerland. He went to the Soviet zone and died there.

Fuchs himself, meanwhile, had been removed from Brixton to Wormwood Scrubs. His special privileges as a prisoner awaiting trial were stopped, and he was put into prison uniform. Three months later, on June 27, he was sent to Stafford gaol in Staffordshire. He never exercised his right of appeal, and he made no effort to have his case reviewed. After this brief passage through the courts—and as a compact and rapid process of law the case was something of a model of its kind—he vanished almost before the public was aware of him though he left behind an enormous field of misgiving and speculation.

Probably not even Fuchs himself could describe the processes of his mind on his arrest, when at least some of his illusions were broken at last. Those who saw him in prison immediately afterward were struck by the improvement in his appearance. He passed the month between his first appearance at Bow Street and his sentence at the Old Bailey in that state of detachment which usually overtakes a man who realises that life as he used to know it has gone for good, and that presently he may be about to die. In an English gaol there was never the remotest possibility of his having to face a lynching party or the real fury of the community. But he was aware of it.

When Skardon saw him after the Bow Street hearing he had

no resentment at his arrest, and, in fact, more than once in the
ensuing few weeks, while he was awaiting trial, he sent for
Skardon to give him further information. He was still not quite
sure that he could give away his contacts in the Russian Intelligence Service, and he was not particularly good at remembering faces and dates and places; still, within these limits he was
ready to help as much as he could. This was part of the atone-
ment for "those other crimes." It is doubtful if Fuchs has ever
admitted to himself the full extent of the harm he has done
society any more than the Germans could be got to admit their
guilt in the last war. But of "those other crimes," of his private
treason, his betrayal of his immediate friends, he was acutely
conscious. He wrote to them at length. Prisoners in British gaols
are not allowed fountain pens, but he did the best he could with
a scratchy prison nib and the unglazed prison notepaper that
blotted badly at times. He wrote in a small, neat hand, and the
grammar and phrasing were precise. No one need doubt the
sincerity of these letters, and they did reveal here and there
that he was going through a moment of truth. He said he had
begun at last—too late—to understand affection. As a boy in
Germany he had always joined himself to other students because
their political beliefs were the same as his own—not because he
liked them or admired them for their own sakes. Friends, then,
were always a means to an end; now he was beginning to see that
that was false and inhuman, and it was not easy for him in his
30's to learn what most others knew when they were 16. He
said he realised that his friends would never want to hear from
him again.

His friends, however, did not desert him. Their first reaction
to the news of the arrest was utter stupefaction. Those whom
he had particularly harmed were people like Professor Peierls
who were themselves originally refugees from Nazi Germany
and who, after a long struggle over many years, had established

themselves in England, and were known as men of great integrity and intelligence. Scientists of the distinction of Professor Peierls were unlikely to be much affected, but it was impossible to avoid feeling that Fuchs had cast suspicion upon them all. As Lord Goddard had suggested, who in England would trust aliens after this? All scientists were hit, and the refugees most of all.

Peierls, however, went to Fuchs in prison, directly he heard the news, to see how he could help to straighten out the mess —for Harwell, for the scientists, for the British, for Fuchs, and for everybody else. There were other visitors, too, all of whom had been undermined in some way by this treachery, and perhaps these painful meetings were the most salutary things that could have happened to Fuchs. For they must have revealed to him that there are people in the world who are always moved by distress, and who still regard friendship as a tie, even when it has been rejected and betrayed. They found him humble, and ready to be reviled. He was not demoralised, but he had no defences left. He expected only punishment. He had no complaints about what was being done to him. One of his women friends saw him in Brixton before the trial when he was still entitled to wear his own clothes, and could buy cigarettes and receive gifts, but she was appalled that he should be in prison at all. She asked him: "Where are you sleeping, what are you getting to eat, what is it like?" He answered, "It's not bad. Old [here he named an acquaintance who had luxurious tastes] would have died a thousand deaths. But it's not bad."

After the trial, when he saw that his friends had not deserted him, he continued to write to them. He said he felt that Lord Goddard had told him what he was bound to hear, and that Curtis-Bennett and others had spoken to him a great deal about arrogance. But was there nothing between abasement and arrogance? Was there no sort of self-respect that he could hope for now, after what had happened? Any schoolboy might have told Klaus Fuchs a great deal about self-respect and arrogance, but this is not a subject that is easy to learn—as Fuchs himself saw —at the age of 38. It is even impossible to learn if one remains fixed in the belief that the individual will is a law to itself and that one's conscience must be one's guide no matter what harm one does to anybody else. In Fuchs' book there was no allowance for the fact that one's conscience may be shining bright while his ignorance of what is right and wrong may be appalling. He had succeeded in utterly confounding Polonius' philosophy that if you are true to yourself then "it must follow as the night the day" you cannot "then be false to any man." Fuchs, according to his lights, had been true to himself, and he had ended up in a welter of falsehood. He deliberately created a double life for himself, the two parts of which were entirely different and contradictory. It was impossible for him to be true to himself because he had *two* selves, each warring against the other. Truth fell down a deep well between these two selves, and it is still to be wondered whether Fuchs has yet succeeded in dredging it up again. The more one contemplates his mind, the more it fades into a limbo of frightful indecision, where the free will becomes chained and determinism becomes free.

With Fuchs in mind it is interesting to read—if only as a literary curiosity—the confession of Doctor Henry Jekyll in Robert Louis Stevenson's *Doctor Jekyll and Mr. Hyde,* for it has certain remarkable resemblances to Fuchs' own confession.

Hence it came about [Doctor Jekyll says] that I concealed my pleasures; and that when I reached years of reflection, and began to look around me and take stock of my progress and position in the world, I stood already committed to a profound duplicity of life. Many a man would have blazoned such irregularities as I was guilty of; but from the high views I set before me, I regarded and hid them with an almost morbid sense of shame. It was thus rather the exacting nature of my aspirations than any particular degradation in my faults, that made me what I was, and, with even a deeper trench than in the majority of men, severed in me those provinces of good and ill which divide and compound man's dual nature. . . . Though so profound a double-dealer, I was in no sense a hypocrite; both sides of me were in dead earnest; I was no more myself when I laid aside restraint and plunged in shame, than when I labored, in the eye of day, at the furtherance of knowledge or the relief of sorrow and suffering. . . .

These and other passages might almost have been put in as evidence by the defence at Fuchs' trial to establish the fact that there is a duality in all men and that the real nature of Fuchs' crime was that he encouraged his duality to the point of treason, and ended in a state of complete confusion. It was no wonder, then, that after his trial, as the weeks in prison went by, he began to search for some way out of the maze by studying philosophy.

He approached philosophy at a gallop, as a boy will plunge into *Robinson Crusoe,* or a bluestocking thirsts after Kafka. First, he began to wonder whether his confession had really accomplished anything at all beyond helping MI 5. It had destroyed him and his relationship with his friends; but nothing seemed to have taken its place. He sent for, and was allowed to have, Kant's *Critique of Pure Reason,* and many books of other philosophers—Greek, German, French, and English. These he absorbed with religious attention and in great quantities, his first real study of philosophy since his student reading of Karl Marx. It produced strange but not unexpected results. He attempted to relate philosophy, especially Kant, to quantum physics.

He read Dickens, and said in a letter to a friend that he was quite bowled over by the opening sentence of *A Tale of Two Cities.* That sentence, an apostrophe on the violent opposites of life in 1775, must indeed have a strong appeal to the schizophrenic mind. It reads:

It was the best of times, it was the worst of times, it was the age of wisdom, it was the age of foolishness, it was the epoch of belief, it was the epoch of incredulity, it was the season of Light, it was the season of Darkness, it was the spring of hope, it was the winter of despair, we had everything before us, we had nothing before us, we were all going direct to Heaven, we were all going direct the other way—in short, the period was so far like the present period, that some of its noisiest authorities insisted on its being received, for good or for evil, in the superlative degree of comparison only.

A world, in fact, where everything was either black or white, and nothing lay in between, and there was no finality anywhere. The world of 1950.

Then, presently, in the gloom of prison, he began to compose poetry, in English, and with a Tennysonian flavour. He wrote much and posted the results off to his friends. Of his own case he wrote less and less. What else was there to say?

To Henry Arnold, the security officer at Harwell, his attitude was: "Don't blame yourself that I deceived you. Blame Stalin, Lenin, Marx, and all the other Communists. I was learning affection at Harwell. I was already changing. I was beginning to see the deep-rooted firmness of the English, and their decent way of life. I would have come to you in the end, whatever happened, and I would have told you what I had done."

There is probably some truth in this, for Fuchs had a deep regard for Arnold. The relationship between the two men is, indeed, an interesting study in the field of counterespionage. Arnold from the first had had a general reservation in his mind about Fuchs. It hardly amounted to a suspicion; he simply felt that if anyone at Harwell was betraying secrets, then it was more likely to be Fuchs than anybody else. So, from 1946 onward, he deliberately cultivated Fuchs' friendship. At first Fuchs did not respond very eagerly, and it was Arnold who had to make all the approaches. Then, little by little, Fuchs began to come round, and by 1949 a genuine intimacy had grown up between them. It was the kind of intimacy—perhaps "trust" is the better word—that exists between opponents who see that they are implacably committed to a duel against each other. Such relationships can be more lucid and enduring than those based on emotional liking, and the familiar enemy becomes at last more trustworthy than the temperamental friend.

By 1949 Fuchs found himself in a hopeless position, for by then he wanted to give up the struggle; he wanted to accept Arnold's friendship *in toto,* and come over to Arnold's side. But he could not bring himself to make an open avowal to his friend of the appalling things he had done. This was the point where Arnold, having to some extent prepared Fuchs for his conversion and confession, handed him over to Skardon; and Fuchs, no doubt, found it a good deal easier to confess to a stranger whom he had not personally betrayed over a long period of time.

And now that it was all over, now that the poison had gathered and burst, Fuchs began to discover that Arnold had no personal bitterness against him. It was Arnold who wound up Fuchs' estate at Harwell. He sold the grey saloon MG car (which Fuchs had bought from Professor Skinner). He disposed of the furniture, the clothes, and the books in "prefab" No. 17; he settled Fuchs' debts and deposited for him the three or four hundred pounds that were left. One thing, however, Arnold could not bring himself to sell or keep; that was a prisoner's uniform with a patch on the back that Fuchs had worn as an internee in Canada. He had kept it all these years in a trunk under his bed. Arnold wrote to Fuchs in prison and told him he proposed to burn it. Fuchs indifferently agreed, and that was one more bit of the past that was gone for good.

The Fuchs case was considered just once again at a public hearing in December 1950, when the Deprivation of Citizenship

Committee debated on whether Fuchs should be deprived of his British citizenship. Fuchs did not exercise his right to appear before the committee, nor was he represented. But he presented a letter in which he argued that there could be little doubt as to where his loyalties now lay. If his citizenship was to be taken away from him as a punishment, then he had nothing to say even though he was already serving the maximum sentence. But he did not think the matter would be regarded as a punishment. He could not ask the Secretary of State to accept from him an assurance of loyalty but he suggested that the opinion of MI 5 and the Director of Public Prosecutions should be obtained. He had made his confession, he said, of his own free will, after Sir John Cockcroft had asked him to resign from Harwell but had offered to retain him as a consultant. He had co-operated loyally with MI 5 and the FBI since his arrest, and he had done this without any threat or promise having been made to him.

Fuchs very much wanted to retain his citizenship. It was clear that he felt that here in England his loyalties had become fixed at last. To distrust him now was to go against the facts. However, when he heard that the authorities were bound by the law, and that they were determined on taking his nationality away, he did not press the matter but he was much distressed. The order went through and was published in the London *Gazette* in February 1951.

These were among the last contacts Fuchs had from prison with the outside world. From time to time there were reports that he was being re-employed on atomic energy research, but this was not so. He remained at Stafford gaol, something of a celebrity among the other prisoners, but with no substantial differences in privileges or treatment. He sewed canvas mail bags. He corresponded less and less with his friends as he sank back into a world where there is no free will, and where the conscience is supplanted by steel bars. He was liked by the other prisoners. Those who emerged from gaol spoke of his quietness, and of his generosity in sharing his cigarettes.

It is a remarkable thing that nearly all the people who came into contact with Fuchs for the first time during the period of his arrest and his trial were immensely impressed by him. They regarded him not as a political imbecile, nor as a charlatan, nor as a criminal anarchist—though he might truthfully have been called by all those names. They thought him very reasonable. Those who knew nothing of his work as a physicist still respected him for his serious intelligence in other matters, and some of them grew to like him very much. It is perhaps all too easy to find virtues in a broken man for no one need be jealous of him any longer. Napoleon on Elba is a much more sympathetic figure than Napoleon at Austerlitz. Fuchs was not a bore nor a boaster nor a coward. It required a certain type of courage to take up his Russian contacts again in England after Nunn May had been caught, and at the time of his investigation he very seriously contemplated suicide. But there are circumstances when it is more difficult to reject suicide than to succumb to it—and this may have been such a case. Fuchs was always governed by his brain, not by his emotions, and there seems to be no reason to doubt him when he says that he realised that suicide would have offered no solution at all, either for himself, or for the people at Harwell, or for anybody else—though just possibly it might have been politically convenient.

But at the time of the trial, and for long afterward, few people were concerned over the personal problems of Fuchs' life, or what he was going to do with it now that he had been caught. He had raised much bigger issues. It seemed to many that treason had come much closer to the ordinary lives of ordinary people than it had ever done before. In the phrase of Rebecca West, "a vast gap had been knocked in the hedge," and who among us was going to be able to trust anyone else, entirely, ever again? In other words, Fuchs had committed the crime society is least able to forgive: he had made society distrust itself. And for that he was hated.

Part Three • BRUNO PONTECORVO

Twelve

•

THE FUCHS CASE SET UP A STIR IN THE UNIVERSITIES AND
laboratories everywhere in Britain for many scientists had known
the prisoner, many were of foreign birth and had had left-wing
views at one time or another. Among those at Harwell who came
to see the security officer, Henry Arnold, was Doctor Bruno
Pontecorvo. This was in February 1950, while the Fuchs trial was
pending.

As part of the ordinary security routine at Harwell, Pontecorvo had been sent a questionnaire that contained queries about
his family—their names, nationalities, and so on. Pontecorvo told
Arnold that he would like to have a private talk about the questionnaire, and in the course of that talk he volunteered the
information that he had a younger brother named Gilberto who
was a Communist. This Gilberto had no connection whatever
with Harwell or with science—he was an Italian citizen living
in Italy; still, Pontecorvo said, he felt security ought to know
about him.

Pontecorvo was something of a figure at Harwell. He had
arrived there less than 18 months before, to take up a post as a
senior principal scientific officer, but in that time he had established himself as one of the most buoyant and likable people
on the station. Atomic scientists are not exceptionally light-

hearted men as a rule, and perhaps Pontecorvo was the more conspicuous because of that. He was always gay. In the words of some of his older colleagues, he was the "Ramon Navarro type": a dark man, of medium height, very good-looking, and with charming, lively manners. He was the extrovert who made friends easily, he flirted mildly at the cocktail parties, and he talked adroitly and well. The Pontecorvos were constantly hard up because he was entirely generous, and careless with his money; he said once that he never counted the notes in his wallet, so that he should not worry if he lost it. He was known to everyone at Harwell as "Ponte" or Bruno.

It is a notable thing that when Nunn May and Fuchs were arrested, and their friends had got over their first astonishment, they looked back and remembered many little things, many oddities in the characters of the two men; and in the end they agreed, yes, they could have been traitors, they could have done it. But in the case of Pontecorvo they are utterly baffled. There seems to have been such an artlessness and frankness about him —his comings and goings were so well-known over so many years —that his friends still cannot bring themselves to accept any really sinister reason for his disappearance. They agree that if a spy must choose a disguise, then this sort of carefree manner would be an excellent one, but they found Pontecorvo's performance too flawless to have been anything but genuine. For them the picture of Pontecorvo as a traitor simply does not fit the facts: it would be just as rational to believe that Einstein was a secret baby killer, or that Stalin was, in reality, a fox-hunting gentleman from the shires.

There were his laziness, his enthusiasms, his occasional irresponsibilities, and above all his tennis. He was a fervent tennis player—much given to dashing up to the net. It was generally understood that he had once won the singles championship of Italy, and before the war he and one of his brothers had played with King Gustav of Sweden on the Riviera. There was, too, his passion for motoring. Soon after his arrival at Harwell he bought himself a new Standard Vanguard, and in this he frisked about the Berkshire downs and he was welcome wherever he went.

No one was led by this happy manner to doubt Pontecorvo's abilities: he was known and respected as a very able scientist indeed, perhaps even the superior of Fuchs in some directions. Fuchs' brain was a machine—a precision instrument that could go on making accurate calculations indefinitely—but it was never thought that he would create some new discovery in physics. About Pontecorvo, though, there was always the feeling that he would turn up with an original work one day—something entirely new and imaginative. The Russians have a way of saying that such and such a man "would never invent a monkey." The difference between Fuchs and Pontecorvo was that Fuchs could never be a monkey inventor, whereas Pontecorvo just conceivably might be one day. Indeed, as far back as 1935, when Pontecorvo was only 22, he signed his name with five other Italian scientists to a paper that appeared in the *Proceedings* of the Royal Society at London. This was entitled "Artificial Radio-activity Produced by Neutron Bombardment," and it is acknowledged now to be something of a milestone in original research.

Physical scientists tend to reach their full powers in their late 30's (after which many of them fade away), and in January 1949, when he first arrived at Harwell, Pontecorvo had just turned 36, and already had a considerable record behind him.

There was just one peculiarity in the background of this brilliant and likable man: that was his wife, Marianne. She seldom, if ever, attended the cocktail parties and the tennis. She stayed at home with the three children—Gil, Tito, and Antonio. She did all the cooking, shopping, and housekeeping for the family. No servant—not even a baby sitter—was ever employed though on Pontecorvo's salary, around £1300 a year, they certainly might have got some help from time to time. Except for relatives who came to stay with them, they hardly ever entertained. They had only two small parties during the whole of their stay at Harwell and their guests were astonished to see how bare and cheerless the house was. The floors were mostly bare. A camp bed, a rocking horse, and a Dutch chair stood in the living room. Only one bedroom was furnished in reasonable comfort, and in the kitchen a modern washing machine seemed a strange extravagance in that Spartan house.

Marianne Pontecorvo had very few friends and when she happened to meet other families at Harwell she was often shy to the point of apparent rudeness. Yet she was a pretty girl. She had gleaming blonde hair, a round Scandinavian face with wide-set eyes and firm mouth, and the figure of a boy. In appearance she was the accepted idea of a Nordic, open-air girl, and one would think that she might have enjoyed the cocktails and the tennis.

It was perhaps nothing remarkable that Marianne should have been so painfully shy, and clearly she loved her husband, and preferred to be with him and the children. But there were people at Harwell who had known the Pontecorvos in Canada during the war, and when the family arrived in England in 1949 they were struck by the change that had come over them. Pontecorvo seemed to have aged somewhat, and very quickly. Marianne's shyness had developed into something a good deal more; it was almost as though she were frightened.

However, these things caused no great comment at Harwell; the family was simply accepted as another odd piece in that complicated jigsaw and a place found for it in the pattern. It was known that Marianne was Swedish, that Pontecorvo was Italian, and that somewhere in the background there was a numerous flock of brothers and sisters in the Pontecorvo family.

On the subject of politics Pontecorvo was a hopeless conversationalist, for he had nothing to say. Like Fuchs, whom he knew slightly but seldom talked to (the Fuchs group, one suspects, was a little too highbrow and too serious for Pontecorvo), he was transfixed by his work. The only other point about him that his colleagues particularly noticed was that he was a mighty job hunter. He had barely arrived at Harwell before he began angling for university chairs in Italy, America, and elsewhere. In the spring of 1950, when he came to see Arnold with his information about his Communist brother, he was inclining toward a job at Liverpool University, where Professor Skinner was then established.

The fact that Fuchs was originally German did not immediately mean that every foreign-born scientist at Harwell came under suspicion. The duty of Arnold and the security officers was to take each case separately on its merits, and with Pontecorvo there was certainly no cause for immediate alarm. He had not been engaged on secret work for some time, nor had he access to the vital experiments at Harwell, though he did see some of the secret papers. The fact that Pontecorvo had a Communist brother was important but it proved nothing. Not having possession of a private army of investigators, British security was in no position to send men running all over Europe to check on the family histories of every scientist employed by the Government. But they could and did go through Pontecorvo's record again, new sources of information opened up, and in the end they were left with a story which was one more object lesson in the fact that the evil of Hitler and Mussolini still lives on and flourishes in the postwar world.

Bruno Pontecorvo was born in Pisa on August 22, 1913. Like Fuchs, he grew up in the midst of war and uncertainty in a provincial town where his family were among the more intellectual people in the community, and like Fuchs, he saw that family become ostracised and disintegrate under the impact of Fascism. The pattern is familiar. But, as one would half expect, things happened more gently under the Italian sun than in Germany, and the story of the Pontecorvos is less drastic, more blessed with compromise and human understanding, than the tragedy of the Fuchses.

The father was Massimo Pontecorvo, born in the 1870's, the mother was Maria, and they were both Jews. Massimo had an interest in several businesses connected with the textile trade, and for a time, his affairs flourished. At all events, he was able to bring up and educate a family of true Italian dimensions. There were eight children and Bruno was the third or fourth. It is necessary to present all these brothers and sisters, like the cast of a play, for they each have some bearing on Bruno's story. They continued in that crowded household in Pisa (in a two-storey building behind a high garden wall, close to the Leaning Tower), the children following one another to school and university, until 1938. Then, with the war impending, and his alliance with Hitler fixed, Mussolini's hand came down on the Jews; Massimo's business began to fail, and the family broke up. This is the point where we can best identify the children by dividing them into two groups—those who came north to England, and those who scattered elsewhere through the world.

Guido, the eldest boy, led the expedition to England. He was then 32, and he had an excellent record as a biologist and a specialist in genetics. He settled in Scotland eventually, became a naturalised British subject shortly after the war, and subsequently joined the Glasgow University staff. In 1939, when things became still more difficult for the family in Pisa, Guido's youngest brother and two of his sisters followed him to Britain. The brother was Giovanni David, and he was only 13 when he arrived. He finished his schooling in Worcester, specialised in agriculture, married an English girl, and became naturalised in 1948.

The two sisters were Anna and Laura. Anna was barely 15 when her arrival was noted by the immigration officers, and although she settled in England she remained an Italian citizen. She was educated at Tunbridge Wells and elsewhere in southern England until soon after the outbreak of war; then she went to Glasgow, and there obtained her Master of Arts degree with second class honours. With a wide knowledge of European languages Anna Pontecorvo has since concentrated on teaching.

Laura Pontecorvo, who was older than Anna, became a naturalised British subject. She too studied in Britain, at first in Birmingham, and then at Edinburgh, where she stayed with Guido for a time. Early in the war she became a probationer nurse at London Hospital, and she continued at various hospitals in London until she qualified as a sister. In February 1950 she joined the staff of the New End Hospital at Hampstead. Seven months later, and about a month after Bruno vanished, she too left England. It was her intention to take up a post in Italy with a society dealing with the care and welfare of children and she went first to Rome, to the house of another sister; and there, so far as is known, she remained.

These four, then, were the British contingent: Guido, the biologist, Giovanni David, the agriculturist, Anna, the teacher, and Laura, the nurse. They are all people of exceptional talent, and though they met Bruno while he was in England, and there were strong ties of affection in this as in every Italian family, no word written here is intended to question their loyalty in any way. None of them has any explanation of Bruno's disappearance.

There remain the other four children, who did not seek refuge in England. These were Bruno (whom we shall come to in a moment), Paul (who went to the United States, and became an American citizen employed on radar research work, and who is least concerned with this story), and finally Gilberto and Giuliana. These last two occupy a central position in these events.

Gilberto Pontecorvo has lived a full life, in not very easy cir-

cumstances, for he was only 20 when war broke out, and there
has been a certain gusto and determination in his activities ever
since. He got into France in November 1939, after studying
science in Pisa, and he plunged at once into wartime journalism
of an extreme leftist hue. He seems to have been undeterred by
the arrival of the Nazis in Paris for he continued working underground for several illegal and anti-Nazi organisations. No doubt
he was able to move about the more freely because he was an
Italian citizen, and therefore presumably an ally of the Germans.
In 1941 he was a member of a clandestine organisation known as
the "Centre d'Action Contre le Facisme," and his particular job
was to act as a liaison between France and Italy. By the end of
1943 he was in charge of the clandestine press of the "Front de la
Jeunesse Italienne." During the German occupation of France he
made frequent trips into Italy, and he used as his headquarters an
apartment at St. Tropez in the south of France. When the libera-
tion came, he returned to Italy and emerged into the open. He
became the general secretary of the Jeunesse Italienne, and
founded in Milan a paper called *The Better Life*. In 1946 he was
back in Paris as a representative of a young Communist organisation, and corresponding with such Italian papers as *Omnibus* and
Milano Sera. Later he was back in Italy, still travelling widely
with his French wife, and concerning himself with an Italian film
company. Gilberto's Communist sympathies have been well-
known and openly expressed in a limited circle for some years
past. In pointing this out to Henry Arnold, Bruno Pontecorvo was
hardly giving away a secret. But it should be noted that until the
Fuchs trial he did not think it worth while to raise the matter with
security.

Giuliana, the eldest daughter, lived in Rome and was married
to Duccio Tabet, a professed Communist. They had three children. Tabet was a scientist on the agricultural staff of the Italian
Communist Party, while Giuliana was an associate of the left-

wing politician Nenni, whom she represented on the committee of the Partisans of Rome.

This, then, is the second group: Paul, the scientist in the United States, Gilberto, the underground worker in France, Giuliana, the wife of the Communist Tabet in Rome, and Bruno. The parents, Massimo and Maria, remained in Italy after the breakup of the family home at Pisa, and subsequently moved to Milan.

There is just one other character who must be added before the cast is complete: that is Emilio Sereni, first cousin of the children. He was a prominent member of the Italian Communist Party. At the end of the war he worked at the Ministry of Interior, and in 1946 he became Minister of Post-War Assistance. The following year he became Minister of Public Works. In the Italian Chamber of Deputies he represented one of the Naples constituencies, and he was a member of the central committee of the Italian Communist Party. Sereni came to England in 1940 as one of the delegates to the Sheffield Peace Conference.

In an exceptionally able family Bruno Pontecorvo was the ablest of all. He passed from his elementary school in Pisa to the Ginnasio and the Classical Liceo, taking all his examinations with ease, and at the age of 16 he entered Pisa University. There he took his two-year certificate in physics and mathematics, and he went on to the University of Rome. He took his doctorate in physics, with honours, in 1934, and continued at Rome University as a research worker and a teacher. His master there was Professor Enrico Fermi, one of the authors of the famous paper on neutron bombardment, and later one of the elite among atomic scientists in the United States. Professor Fermi remembered Pontecorvo as a very likable student of great promise. Probably Professor Fermi and other scientists in that brilliant group in Rome had a hand in getting Pontecorvo a national fellowship in 1936. With this Pontecorvo went to Paris in February 1936 and he enrolled himself as a student at the Collège de France.

He took rooms at 17, Place du Pantheon, and there he met Marianne. Under her maiden name of Helene Marianne Nordblom she also had come to Paris to study. She was four years younger than Pontecorvo. They lived together and on July 30, 1938, their first son Gil was born.

By this time Pontecorvo was working under Professor Frédéric Joliot-Curie at the Institute of Radium in Paris, and when the war broke out he was a research associate at the Laboratory of Nuclear Chemistry at the Collège de France. There was a vigorous left-wing movement among students in Paris then but it is not known that Pontecorvo took any active part in it. He said that he had come to study in France because it was difficult for a scientist to progress under Mussolini, and it seems likely that he was much more anti-Fascist than pro-Communist.

He had travelled in Europe fairly widely. There was a week's holiday in England in 1935, and in the summer of 1939 he made a tour of the physical laboratories in Scandinavia, the Low Countries, and Switzerland. At the outbreak of war Pontecorvo made no attempt to return to Italy. He continued to work in Paris through the cold war period, and on January 9, 1940, he and Marianne were married. They were overtaken the following summer by the German break-through. An Italian can hardly have been popular in France at that moment, even under the protection of the incoming Nazi troops, and the Pontecorvos joined in the general flight from Paris to the south. On June 29, when Pétain had already sought for armistice terms, Pontecorvo applied for an exit permit to enable him to go to the United States, and then the family set out—Marianne and the baby by train and Pontecorvo on a bicycle—for Toulouse. Here they joined Duccio and Giuliana Tabet, who had come up from Italy, and the whole party continued southward into Spain. On July 24, coming from Madrid, they crossed from Spain into Portugal, and on August 9 they boarded the SS *Oranza* bound for the United

States. For some curious reason, the Tabets declared to the authorities in Portugal that they were medical doctors, and later that they were engaged in commerce.

The *Oranza*, a neutral ship, took eleven days on the crossing and on August 20—two days before Pontecorvo's 27th birthday— the party disembarked at New York. Pontecorvo's first concern was to find a job. Through his university connections he obtained an introduction to the Wells Survey, Inc., of Tulsa, Oklahoma, which employed him as a consultant on radiographic oil-well logging. It was while Pontecorvo was working in Oklahoma that he developed improvements in the system of oil logging, and filed an application for a patent on his invention. Meanwhile the atomic energy project was getting under way in the United States and Canada and Professor Fermi and others, who knew of Pontecorvo's abilities, were already in the United States. Presently Pontecorvo's name was put forward to the British authorities, and early in 1943—at the time Nunn May crossed the Atlantic from England—Pontecorvo was invited to join the Anglo-Canadian Research team at Montreal. At this time he still held an Italian passport, but he had filed first papers for United States naturalisation in 1941. From this time forward until he vanished Pontecorvo lived in a whirl of indecision about what nationality he should finally settle on. Throughout he seems to have been greatly influenced by the various jobs that were offered him, and at any moment he was quite ready to change his nationality if the job required it.

On their way north the family stayed briefly in New York and Montreal, and then, when work on the Chalk River heavy-water pile began, they moved out to the nearby settlement of Deep River. There they remained for the next six years. Pontecorvo's official record during these six years is quite direct and simple. He was well liked by the other scientists, he worked extremely hard at the heavy-water pile, and when the war was

over he was asked to stay on as a member of the British Ministry
of Supply and help in further experimentation in Canada. Before he came to Canada, and again on this occasion, he was examined by security officials, and they found nothing against him.
He was examined a third time early in 1948, when he applied
for and was granted British nationality. During this period he
made a number of visits to the United States, usually in connection with his work, and once he made a private trip to Italy,
calling at England on the way. By now his reputation was so
firmly established that he was offered a senior position at Harwell. He accepted, and crossed from Canada to England early
in 1949. At no point had security any complaint about him. He
was known as a man who never talked politics, not even atomic
politics, and his associations were all with men of established
loyalty in scientific work in North America.

That was the official record. The private and domestic life
of the Pontecorvos was much more complicated. A second son
was born in Canada on March 20, 1944, and given the curious
name of Tito Nils. The third son, Antonio, was born in July
the next year. On Pontecorvo's pay and allowances the family
was able to live at Deep River not expansively, but adequately.
They had their house, Pontecorvo was a member of a car club,
and he drove off each day to his work at the laboratories at
Chalk River. In his spare time he played tennis and won the
local singles championship. Marianne was regarded as a rather
difficult woman to get on with in the settlement, but she did not
appear to be unhappy. Just once there was a domestic crisis which
nearly broke up the marriage, and revealed how much Marianne
was in love.

This was in June 1947, when Pontecorvo set off with a colleague on one of his official visits to Montreal. They offered a
ride in the car to two attractive girls, and when their work at
Montreal was over they continued on across the border to Boston

—taking the girls along. Marianne was deeply affronted when she heard of this. She went to her bank and withdrew $1,800, which was probably the entire credit balance. She then got on the 4 A.M. transcontinental train to Banff in the Rockies, taking the children with her. When Pontecorvo got back from Boston he found the house empty and Marianne had left no address. It was then Pontecorvo's turn to feel desperate and he became increasingly so as the days went on with no word from his family. At length friends phoned to Marianne at Banff and persuaded her to come back.

Then there was Pontecorvo's unofficial correspondence with various universities in America and abroad. It would be tedious to follow all the many negotiations he entered into immediately after the war, when he was trying to make up his mind whether or not to become British and continue as a civil servant. A list of the jobs he was offered indicates how much he was in demand. In 1945 he was offered an associate professorship at a radiation laboratory in Massachusetts at $6,000 a year; both the General Electric Company in Schenectady and the radiation laboratory at Berkeley, California, invited him to make a visit with a view to taking up an appointment; and the University of Michigan at Ann Arbor offered him a full professorship at $5,000 a year.

In 1947 there were two more offers: one, a chair in experimental physics at the Hebrew University, Jerusalem, and the other an associate professorship at Cornell University at $7,000 a year. All through this period Pontecorvo kept making trips across the border to the United States at six-month intervals so that he could establish his residence there in case he eventually decided to become an American citizen.

But in December 1947 he made a trip to Europe and this appears to have decided him at last. In all their years in North America both Pontecorvo and Marianne had had a nostalgia for Europe, especially for Paris, and no doubt this journey revived that feeling even though it meant a considerable financial loss in turning down the American offers.

Pontecorvo came alone to England on December 8, 1947 and stayed at Abingdon, near Harwell, with some old friends from his wartime days at Chalk River, Doctor and Mrs. Henry Seligman. At Harwell he was told that a post would be made available for him, and he renewed his contract with the British Ministry of Supply. He flew on then to Milan to see his parents, intending to return to England and embark on the *Aquitania* for New York on January 4, 1948. He came back from Italy by train, paused in Paris to meet some of his friends on New Year's Eve, and missed the boat. He then flew to America on January 6. On his return to Canada he was reminded that mid-April was the last opportunity for filing his second papers for United States naturalisation. But by now his mind was fully made up: he wanted to get back to Europe, and he wanted to continue in government research work. In February 1948, while still in Canada, he became a British subject, and in January 1949 the whole family set off for Harwell.

They stayed at first with the Seligmans until a house was found for them close by, in Letcombe Avenue on the Fitzharry estate in Abingdon. They were now surrounded by Pontecorvo's brothers and sisters in England; Marianne was able to visit her parents in Sweden, a school was found for the children, and it seemed to their friends that they were beginning to settle down. But it was not the end of Pontecorvo's restlessness. In May 1949 he lectured in Paris at the invitation of Joliot-Curie, he visited Brussels, he negotiated for some additional work with the Anglo-Iranian Oil Company, and in September he went off with several other Harwell scientists to a nuclear physics conference at Lake Como in Italy (they overstayed their leave in that happy place). And he continued doggedly with his job hunting. There were two vacant chairs of experimental physics in Italy—one in Rome and the other in Pisa—and he seriously intended to enter for them. He acquired a medical certificate of sound health from Milan, a penal certificate from Pisa, stating that no convictions were recorded against him, and a copy of his birth certificate—all required of candidates for the two chairs. He discussed these matters with Arnold, saying that if he were successful he would have to revert to Italian nationality. Arnold reminded him that he had only just become a British citizen, and that perhaps it was a little wearing for a man to be constantly shifting about from one nationality to another. In the end Pontecorvo took neither job; his Pisa application arrived too late, and he abandoned his application to Rome when Professor Skinner came forward with the proposal from Liverpool.

And now it was the early spring of 1950 when the Fuchs trial was disturbing scientists everywhere, and Pontecorvo came to Arnold with his admission that his brother Gilberto was a Communist. The two men met again a few days later and Arnold then asked him if it was a fact that, during his recent trip to Lake Como, he had met this brother Gilberto. Pontecorvo seemed rather taken aback at this, but he admitted it readily and he went on to say that there were other members of his family who were Communists—or at any rate sympathetic to Communism.

There began from that moment a different relationship between Pontecorvo and Wing Commander Arnold at Harwell. Without there being any obvious signs, Pontecorvo clearly regarded himself as under suspicion and his manner was not always as lighthearted as it used to be. Indeed Pontecorvo was no longer *persona grata* for early in March a report on him had arrived from Sweden which made it clear that both Pontecorvo and Marianne were Communists. There was nothing to support this in England or in Canada, but it was evident that from now on he would have to be closely watched. It was about this time that Pontecorvo seriously began to consider joining

Skinner at Liverpool. He made a trip there with his wife and the children, and they were shown a university apartment which would be made available for them. Correspondence with the authorities was begun—but still Pontecorvo hesitated. He was deeply impressed with the Liverpool laboratories, and the new cyclotron for atomic research which was then rising on consecrated ground originally intended for a Roman Catholic cathedral, but Marianne was worried about the cold in the north. At length Skinner wrote him that there came a time when all considerations had been considered, and there was nothing to consider any longer except yes or no. On this Pontecorvo accepted, and it was arranged that he should take up the appointment in Liverpool in January 1951.

In June there was a brief trip to Cornwall which the Pontecorvos made with Guido Pontecorvo and his wife and another friend. Then the family set about planning their summer holiday in Italy. They were to go by car, starting July 25, 1950, and Anna, the sister who was a teacher, was to go with them. They were to cross the Channel by car ferry, and then drive south in easy stages to northern Italy, where there would be a reunion with their parents, Massimo and Maria. With three children and three adults there was not much room for luggage in the Standard Vanguard, and it was agreed that each should take the barest essentials. They intended to sleep out, and Pontecorvo had bought a quantity of expensive camping equipment. His friends were a little puzzled at this, because they had offered to lend him all the canvas beds and tents he needed, but he insisted on having his own. There was one other incident: a friend of the Pontecorvos had some francs in France, and it was arranged that Pontecorvo should pick these up on his way through. It was only a small sum, and the friend did not know the precise amount so he suggested that the matter should be settled between them on Pontecorvo's return. Pontecorvo, however, insisted on giving him a blank cheque in advance.

Security at Harwell was well aware of Pontecorvo's departure but had not sufficient reason and no legal power to prevent his going. A naturalised British subject enjoys all the privileges of a natural-born Briton, and one of the most definite of those privileges is that he may move about in peacetime wherever he pleases.

Nothing of any consequence happened through the rest of June and July. It was accepted that Pontecorvo should be back in England for a conference in early September and that thereafter he would move on to Liverpool. Just before the family set off, Mrs. Seligman had a final game of tennis with Pontecorvo. As they came off the court he made a solemn and unexpected remark: "We'll play again someday."

There was also a small farewell party at the Seligmans' house which was only a few doors away from the Pontecorvos'. During the party Marianne went off in a corner by herself. She picked up a copy of the magazine *Vogue* and seemed to be reading it. After a time Mrs. Seligman went over to her and found that, in fact, she was not reading. She had buried her face in the magazine and she was in tears. Pontecorvo professed to be annoyed at this but the incident passed off, and he took his wife home.

The following day the family set off for the Continent, leaving all their heavy clothes and almost everything else they possessed locked up in their house at Abingdon.

Thirteen

•

MOST BRITISH MOTORISTS WHO MAKE FOR THE MEDITERRANEAN IN
the summer follow a route which has been established for many
years, and their movements are almost as regular as those of the
migratory birds. Once they land in France they head directly
south toward the sun, usually on Route Nationale No. 6, which
takes them through the vineyards of Burgundy, and then down
the Rhone Valley to the Côte d'Azur. It is a two- or three-day
drive as a rule, and most people plan the journey and book their
accommodations long in advance.

The progress of the Pontecorvo family across Europe in this
summer of 1950 did not conform to any of these rules; indeed,
it can only be described as haphazard. Pontecorvo was not the
man to book hotels or anything else in advance. He loathed writing letters and making precise arrangements—he preferred to
turn up at a place in his own good time and trust to luck. He
was hungry for the sun, and beyond making a few vague appointments to see his friends and his family in Italy, he was
prepared to go where the roads and the weather took him.

He succeeded in getting the Standard aboard a car ferry on
the Channel on the afternoon of July 25, and they landed at
Dunkirk. They then proceeded through Arras and Dijon in
France, and crossed into Switzerland at Neuchâtel after a slow

journey of three days. They took three more days to traverse Switzerland, and arrived at Menaggio on Lake Como on July 31. Here they camped until August 4, when Anna Pontecorvo left them, taking the boat down the lake on her way to see her parents in Milan. At Menaggio the Pontecorvos fell in with Professor Caldirola, a scientist of Padua University, and his wife. A friendship started quickly and Pontecorvo invited Professor Caldirola to come to the unclassified conference in England on September 7. Caldirola agreed. Then, on August 6, Bruno and Marianne decided to visit the Dolomites, and they crossed into Austria for two days. The holiday was going well. Marianne sent off a postcard from Landeck, Vorarlberg, to a friend in Canada, saying that they were having a wonderful time, and that they would be away "another two or three weeks before returning"—presumably meaning to England.

Next the family drove south. They called on Bruno's parents in Milan on August 12 and, still at a leisurely pace, they reached Ladispoli, a seaside place on the Tyrrhenian Sea near Rome, on August 17. Here they had a rendezvous with Giuliana Tabet and her family of small children. The Tabets had returned from the United States sometime previously, and Giuliana had taken a house at Ladispoli for the summer. In this house the two families remained together for a few days until Bruno and Marianne decided to drive south again in search of a coast where he could engage in underwater fishing with a helmet and a spring gun—a sport for which he had developed a passion during the previous summer. They left the youngest child, Antonio, with Giuliana Tabet at Ladispoli and with the other two children continued in the car another sixty or seventy miles down the coast until they reached Circeo, where they set up camp. Circeo is a lovely place on a headland just south of Anzio, where the Allies landed for their final attack on Rome during the war. The legendary Circe is supposed to have lived on Mount Circeo, and beneath the sea and below the mountain there are Roman ruins and a temple to the sun: an ideal seascape for submarine fishing.

Apart from their camping kit they had very little baggage— two small waterproof army satchels, a floppy zippered bag for their clothes, and a small zippered brief case which Bruno always kept close to him. Usually it was placed in the side pocket of the car while they were driving in order to stop the children from playing with it. It contained towels, shaving soap, and Bruno's razor.

Before he left England Bruno had planned to stop for a few days at Chamonix on his return journey since his parents were intending to spend their holidays there. He confirmed this arrangement with his parents when he was in Milan, and now, while he and Marianne were still at Circeo, a new proposal came up which made the plan still more feasible. There is an international scientific laboratory at Chamonix with which Harwell is connected, and which deals with cosmic rays. Knowing that Bruno intended to go to Chamonix in any case, Doctor Bretscher, who was Bruno's chief at Harwell, now sent him a wire suggesting he should call at the laboratory. This wire was sent in two copies—one in care of Bruno's parents in Milan, and the other in care of Professor Amaldi in Rome—on August 20, and Bruno received it at Circeo a few days later.

On August 22, Bruno's 37th birthday, Gilberto Pontecorvo and his French wife, Henriette, arrived at Circeo from Rome, and they had with them Anna Pontecorvo, who had now come south from Milan. All three spent the night at Circeo and returned to Rome on the following day, leaving Bruno, Marianne, and the two children still camping.

This seems to have been the beginning of the crisis in Bruno's affairs. Up to this point there is a certain happy-go-lucky holiday atmosphere in the account of the family's comings and goings. They behaved as tens of thousands of other holiday makers do

in Italy in the month of August, living idly by the warm sea,
and if there was any strain or apprehension or fear in their minds,
then there is no evidence of it from Bruno's correspondence or
from anyone who met them at that time. But after this visit of
Gilberto on August 22 everything changed. The holiday began
to go wrong and Bruno's movements became erratic. It was on
the following day that he had an accident in his car. It was
nothing serious—he collided with a cyclist. Colliding with cyclists
in Italy, especially in midsummer when they appear on the roads
in millions, is almost a routine matter. No one seems to have
been hurt but Bruno decided to drive the car up to Rome to
be repaired: it was only a journey of an hour or two. He left
the car in Rome and returned to Circeo to find that the children
had developed sunstroke—hardly a surprising thing after their
years in the faint sun of Canada and England. Bruno sent off a
telegram to his parents in Milan saying he was sorry, but owing
to the accident to his car and the illness of the children, he
would not now be able to join them in France. No sooner had
he sent this telegram than he got a postcard from his parents
saying that they had already left for Chamonix. Bruno then
wrote a letter to follow his telegram. "As soon as the children
are well enough," he wrote, "we shall return to England. It is
not possible to come to Chamonix as we shall have no time, and
it would tire the children." This letter was posted from Rome
on August 25—for by now they had abandoned their camping
holiday. The children were all gathered together again at Ladispoli and on August 27 Bruno took them up to Rome.

A formidable household of guests now gathered at Giuliana's
small house at Via Gabi, 40, near St. John Lateran in Rome.
There were, in addition to Giuliana's own family, the five Pontecorvos and Gilberto and his wife and Anna. Since there was
no bed for him in the house Bruno slept in the back seat of
the Standard, which had now been repaired. He woke in the

morning feeling cramped and out of spirits; indeed, none of them can have been very comfortable, for the temperature of Rome can be unbearable at the end of August, especially in a small house with six young children in it. Antonio, the youngest child, did in fact have a heat stroke. It was in this atmosphere of noise, confusion, and heat that Bruno proceeded to the decision which nobody has succeeded in explaining yet.

On Tuesday, August 29, he appeared with Marianne at the booking office of the Scandinavian Airways System and enquired about the fares and the times of departure for a flight to Stockholm. He then booked five single tickets—his own in the name of Pontecorvo and the other four for Marianne and the three children in the name of Nordblom-Pontecorvo. He was in the midst of these arrangements when Marianne, who was visibly agitated and miserable, pulled him away from the desk out of earshot of the booking clerk. They had a short conversation and then Bruno returned to the desk and asked that his own ticket should be made into a return. The other tickets were to remain one way and Marianne and the children were to travel on Marianne's Swedish papers. Bruno was told that it was customary for reservations to be confirmed and paid for on the same day but he asked for a delay until the next day—August 30. Throughout the conversation Bruno appeared to be quite unconcerned.

He returned to the booking office next day to confirm and pay, bringing with him the required amount in Italian lire. He was then told that foreigners with less than six months' residence in Italy were obliged to pay in American dollars. At this Bruno expressed surprise and annoyance. However he went off and came back two or three hours later bringing with him a quantity of American dollars. The fares amounted to $602 and he paid in $100 notes, which are something of a rarity in Rome except among the wealthier American tourists. On this second visit to the booking office he was alone.

The following day, August 31, he wrote a postcard to Harwell and it was received there on September 4. It read:

Had a lot of fun with submarine fishing but I had plenty of car trouble. I will have to postpone my arrival until first day of conference [September 7]. Can you tell E. Bretscher? Hope everybody has prepared his talk and done good work at Chamonix. I am sorry I have missed Chamonix but I could not make it. Goodbye everybody. Bruno.

It is confirmed that this postcard, which was of course written when he had no intention of returning, was in his own handwriting.

In the early hours of the following morning the family boarded the SAS plane and flew to Munich, in the American zone of Germany. There they remained in the plane until it took off again for Denmark. From Copenhagen they flew on to Stockholm, arriving at ten minutes to nine at night on the same day. At the airport Bruno made enquiries about accommodation for the night but the family failed to turn up at either of the two hotels where rooms had been promised him. Marianne made no attempt to get in touch with her parents, who lived only a short distance from the airfield, and it is not known where the family spent the night. It has been reported, but not confirmed—and here we are beginning to move into an area where we pass from proven facts to reports and finally into mystery—that the Pontecorvos spent the night at a house belonging to the Soviet Embassy at Stockholm.

The next day, September 2, they reappeared at the airfield, and took the plane to Helsinki in Finland. At the Helsinki airfield Bruno filled out a form in which he stated that the reason for his visit was "tourism," that the length of his stay would be about one week, and he gave his place of residence as "Hotel." A customs official at the Helsinki airfield has said that just be-

fore the Pontecorvos arrived a man and woman came to the
airfield and said they were waiting for the family. They asked
that the Pontecorvos' luggage be placed, not in the airways coach,
but in their car. On their arrival the Pontecorvos got into the
car, and that was the last that was heard of them this side of
the Iron Curtain.

There have been many clues to the family's movements here-
after, impossible to confirm or deny. According to one of these,
the Soviet ship *Bellostov*, which was due to sail from Helsinki
at 10.40 A.M. on September 2, delayed its departure until 5 P.M.,
when the Pontecorvos came on board. The ship was due to
reach Leningrad September 5. Certainly the Finnish authorities
have no record of the Pontecorvos having left Finland—and a
record would exist unless they were travelling with diplomatic
passports. It should perhaps be noted that much the easiest
method for the Pontecorvos to reach Russian territory would
have been for them to drive directly from the airfield across the
border. In a Russian diplomatic car they could have crossed into
Russia unobserved.

At Harwell there was no great concern when Pontecorvo failed
to turn up September 7, the opening day of the conference. It
was remembered that he was notoriously a man who arrived
late, especially when he had been on holiday. There had been
the time when he failed to catch the *Aquitania* when he was
returning to Canada. In the previous summer at the Lake Como
conference it was Pontecorvo who forced the rest of the Harwell
party to overstay their leave. They had only a week's official leave
after the conference but Pontecorvo (who was driving his own
car) had urged the party farther and farther south until they
had reached Rome; and even then he had tried to get them to
go on to Naples. It was remembered, too, that he had had car
trouble.

Professor Caldirola arrived for the conference, looked in vain for Pontecorvo, left a note for him, and departed. The postman kept dropping letters into the house at Letcombe Avenue, but it remained locked and deserted. On September 21 the enquiries began.

In Rome Giuliana Tabet said that as far as she could remember the Pontecorvos had stayed with her until September 6, when they had left very early in the morning, saying that they intended to return to England by easy stages. In mid-September, however, she had had a letter from Bruno which gave her the impression that he was still in Rome. This letter asked her to pay the garage expenses on the car and send it back to England. The car, in fact, was found by the police at the Esso Garage in the Piazza Verde in Rome. Its license and other papers were missing.

Neither Giuliana nor anyone else had any explanation for the family's disappearance. Bruno had appeared to them to be perfectly normal, and he had never mentioned to anybody that he had any plans other than those of returning to England.

Anna Pontecorvo was no more help. She said she had last seen the family at her sister's house in Rome on August 28, and that everything seemed normal with them then. She herself had left Rome for England on the 7.30 A.M. train on August 29.

At Stockholm Marianne's parents were astonished to hear that the family had passed through Sweden without getting in touch with them. They had been writing to England, sending greetings for Gil's birthday, and had been mystified at getting no answer. Bruno's parents, Massimo and Maria Pontecorvo, had been writing to England too, saying they were worried at the lack of news and begging for a reply.

When the house at Abingdon was opened and searched, still nothing of value came to light. It remained precisely as the Pontecorvos had left it except for the dust and the unopened letters that had arrived after their departure. These letters were nothing more than some bills, the birthday greetings for Gil, an insurance policy, and other routine correspondence. There was, however, a letter dated September 11 from Laura Pontecorvo in Rome saying that she was negotiating for a post in Italy; and to this Giuliana had attached a postscript in which she asked what she should do with the property the Pontecorvos left behind: send it back to England? Or keep it until they returned to Italy another time? All the heavy clothing, and one or two valuable personal things which one would have supposed would be useful in Russia, were still in the cupboards at the house. No one at Harwell had any news, or any explanation.

When the story reached the press on October 20, 1950, and reporters in Italy, America, England, Sweden, and Finland set themselves on the trail, there was still nothing new to be learned. One man said he was a passenger on the Pontecorvos' plane to Helsinki and that little Antonio, the youngest boy, had announced during the flight that they were going to Russia. The boy kept looking out of the window and asking, "Is that Russia?" Someone else reported a conversation Bruno had had at Menaggio, in the course of which he said he dared not go back to England. In the House of Commons, Mr. Strauss, the Minister of Supply, was pressed for details. When had the enquiries begun? Why was it not known all along that Bruno was a Communist? What had been done to prevent his leaving the country? What documents had he taken in that zippered brief case? But the Minister was not then able to say definitely that the Pontecorvos were in Russia. Nor was it until several years later that the Russians disclosed that the Pontecorvos had in fact arrived and that Bruno was engaged in scientific work in the Soviet Union.

The house at Abingdon has been rented to other scientists now, the Pontecorvos' furniture has been dispersed among other members of the family, and life at Harwell has closed over the gap left by the Pontecorvos as though they never existed. But the gap is there, nevertheless—an unpleasant-sounding hollow in the minds of everyone who knew and liked Bruno so well.

Some of the more obvious theories can be dismissed quickly. It seems wholly unlikely that the Pontecorvos suddenly decided when in Rome to visit Marianne's parents at Stockholm and were then kidnaped. Despite Marianne's tears on her departure from Abingdon, despite her depression, it seems equally hard to think that they left England intending never to return. So much was left behind, not only in the house—Pontecorvo left £165 in his English bank account, Marianne had £52 in a post office savings book, and Pontecorvo had a credit balance of $1,714 at the Bank of Montreal at Deep River, Ontario. The beginning of their holiday was so casual—so much like a holiday. Moreover, Bruno can hardly have been so heartless as to arrange a meeting with his mother and father at Chamonix when he did not intend to go there. He surely decided not to go to Chamonix only after he had seen Gilberto on August 22, after his car accident and after the children became ill.

It seems much more likely that something happened to Pontecorvo in Italy between August 22 and his disappearance ten days later: something that made him suddenly change his mind and go to Helsinki. And there were people in Rome who knew more about it than they have yet revealed, for Pontecorvo was able at a moment's notice to produce a fairly large sum of American dollars.

If that point is accepted, then two theories present themselves. First, he was a spy of long standing. He may have passed information when the war was on, when Russia was our ally, and many people regarded Russia in a very different light to the one they have now. Perhaps he had signed a receipt for a small sum of money. Then, on arriving at Harwell, he observes that he is under suspicion, even though he is not engaged in secret work. He grows afraid. Marianne breaks down at the farewell party. When they reach Rome he meets agents of the Russian Intelligence through Communist members of his family, and he is invited to go to Russia. It is pointed out to him that he is no longer much use as an agent in England since he has accepted a post on nonsecret work at Liverpool. He is warned that if he refuses to go he will be exposed to the British. So he collects the dollars from the Russians, boards the plane for the north, and disappears.

In support of this theory we have reason to believe that someone, in addition to Fuchs and the other spies who have been arrested, was giving atomic information to the Russians. It could have been Pontecorvo even though he was never detected, and to this day no evidence against him has been uncovered. His name was never mentioned in the Canadian spy case, and Gouzenko knows nothing of him. On the other hand, we know that he was not agitated when he booked his ticket. Marianne was disturbed, but then she had been in a disturbed state of mind for a long time, and the explanation of that may be that Pontecorvo was not a very easy husband. There were quarrels from time to time.

The second theory is that Pontecorvo was not a spy at all. He may have been concerned that suspicion was falling on him at Harwell because of his Communist family background, but in fact his own conscience was clear. When he arrives at Rome, however, the Communists begin to talk to him. They point out that far greater opportunities exist for him in Russia, more money, more scope, more authority; and Russia has need of him. Pontecorvo (largely, perhaps, because of his wife) has been none too keen for the Liverpool job—he has always been ready to go anywhere and take any nationality in order to get ahead. This seems a wonderful opportunity. He is naïve and gullible. He accepts.

As a corollary to this second theory it is also suggested that the Communists in Rome did no more than urge him that he should have a meeting with Russian scientists at Helsinki or in Russia to discuss perhaps some outstanding discovery in the field of cosmic rays—and that once in Russia he was kidnaped. But this seems unlikely.

There is no clear explanation of why Pontecorvo should have booked a return ticket for himself to Rome. He was due to return not to Italy, but to Harwell. It is just possible, of course, that he really did intend to do no more than have a brief meeting with the Russians in the north and then return to Rome to pick up the car and drive it back to England. Marianne and the children could have stayed with her parents in Stockholm or returned direct to England by air. But why, then, did Marianne not get in touch with her parents? Why did she deliberately avoid them and fly on to Helsinki? Alternatively it is possible that the return ticket was nothing more than a red herring meant to confuse the airline company should any enquiries be made about him.

One can go on indefinitely putting forward new possibilities and alternatives but the last two theories, which both presuppose that Pontecorvo was coerced or induced in Rome, seem to come nearest to fitting the facts. In the end one is forced to leave the mystery unsolved and concentrate on the other major aspect of the case. How much use could Pontecorvo be to the Russians? In the way of immediate information there was not much that he could have passed on. He knew about the Canadian heavy-water pile at Chalk River. He knew something of the nuclear problems connected with plutonium piles in the United States. But all his knowledge on these matters was years old and there is every reason to believe that the Russians were already in possession of it. All Pontecorvo's recent researches had little to do with the atomic bomb, and he could not have done much more than confirm what the Russians already knew of the work at Harwell.

It seems much more likely that his chief value to the Russians lies in his skill. Professor Fermi commented after his disappearance: "My impression is that if he went to Russia he may not be able to contribute to their work by the things that he has learned during his connection with the Canadian and the English projects, but rather through his general scientific competence. His knowledge of the use of radioactive methods in prospecting for uranium and oil might be very valuable to the Russians."

Pontecorvo was an experimental physicist—a member of a much larger group than the theoretical physicists. Among experimental physicists he is rated in the first flight. Russia is known to have many such men already, but with Pontecorvo there was always the feeling that there were great possibilities ahead of him.

There is a human quality about his story so far as we know it, an absence of fanaticism and moral gloom, that sets it apart from the records of the general run of the traitors. Somehow one feels deeply for Marianne on that long flight to the north with her three small children. How tired and cross they must have been when they got to Stockholm, only to have to fly on again the next day. How pathetic the stranding of the parents at Chamonix, the abandoned car in the Piazza Verde, the submarine fishing at Circeo, the birthday greetings that Gil never received, Antonio's heat stroke in the Via Gabi in Rome, and the tennis rackets and the washing machine in the deserted house at Abingdon.

These things have no place in the cold world of nuclear physics. But they are the measure of what a man is willing to give up when he has a fixed idea in his mind.

The Summing Up

•

THOSE, THEN, ARE THE CASE HISTORIES OF THE THREE SCIENTISTS
who have done incalculable harm to Britain and perhaps all other
countries this side of the Iron Curtain: Allan Nunn May, the
Englishman, who has never publicly recanted, and who says he
acted as he did for the safety of mankind; Klaus Fuchs, the German, who thought at one time the Russians were building a new
world in which he wanted to play a part and who later said he
was wrong (although he has since contradicted this); and Bruno
Pontecorvo, the Italian, who simply vanished without a word. It
remains now to try and estimate just what damage they actually
did, to understand their motives in doing it, and to see what
measures can be taken to prevent such traitors from getting hold
of our secrets ever again.

In the spring of 1951 the United States Joint Congressional
Committee on Atomic Energy published a pamphlet on the
atomic spies,* and it had this to say about the nature of the
information these men gave the Russians:

Whereas the wartime atomic partners, America, Britain, and Canada,
overcame immense obstacles to construct reactors and to produce

* *Soviet Atomic Espionage,* U. S. Government Printing Office, Washington,
1951.

205

precious fissionable materials, a major share of their experience—thanks
to the spies—was at hand for Russia to exploit without the independent
exertion on her part otherwise necessary. Our own country, striking
into the unknown, felt compelled to build three separate plants for
U-235 production, each based upon a different process.

One of these, a gaseous diffusion method, proved to be far superior,
and since the war has been used almost exclusively. It is the same
method to which Klaus Fuchs had access during the wartime research
and development phase. Here again the Soviets, from an early point in
their effort, could avoid making many of the mistakes and following
many of the costly false leads that inevitably attended the pioneering
days of the American program.

The same point can be made as regards the heavy-water reactor
at Chalk River, Canada. This is all apart from Fuchs' knowledge of
American plans for postwar development, both as to atomic weapons
and as to the hydrogen bomb.

Thus the conclusion seems reasonable that the combined activities
of Fuchs, Pontecorvo, Greenglass, and May have advanced the Soviet
atomic energy program by 18 months as a minimum. In other words,
if war should come, Russia's ability to mount an atomic offensive
against the West will be greatly increased by reason of these four
men. It is hardly an exaggeration to say that Fuchs alone has influenced the safety of more people and accomplished greater damage
than any other spy, not only in the history of the United States
but in the history of nations. This is not to imply that Russia could
never have broken the American atomic monopoly through her own
unaided labors. But if, for example, the United States had known
early in World War II what Russia learned by the end of 1945
through espionage, it appears likely that our own project would today
be at least 18 months ahead of its actual level of development.

The validity of this statement depends, of course, on whether
we have another war in which atomic bombs are used, and upon
the timing of that war. Clearly if the war were to be delayed
another ten or twenty years, the initial start given to the Russians
becomes of increasingly less importance. Clearly, too, there is a

possibility that atomic bombs might not be used in a third World War, just as poison gas was not used in World War II, though this is not a possibility to be counted on. And in any event it probably depends on our having a stockpile of more and better bombs than the Russians.

The technical nature of the atomic bomb is beyond the scope of this book, but there are certain general observations which ought to be made, because there has been great misconception about the atomic spies and the nature of the information they gave away.

In the first place, it was never within the power of Fuchs or anybody else to give the Russians the atomic bomb, and so the importance of Fuchs may be exaggerated in the American statement. The manufacture of the bomb depends entirely on the existence of great industrial and technical resources and of a body of trained scientists and technicians. These the Russians possessed; therefore, as the statement suggests, they would doubtless have produced atomic bombs without any outside help. The most valuable single piece of knowledge they got from America was that the bomb could be made and exploded, and that knowledge they got without the help of traitors.

None of this in the least excuses Fuchs or the other traitors: if they contributed any additional help at all to the Russian effort they were criminals. But it is useful to get this point into perspective if we are going to estimate the damage that has been done.

The next point that has to be faced is that there is a strong possibility that there are other traitors, just as important as Fuchs, who may still be at large. The Canadian spy network was uncovered only by the accident of Gouzenko's defection. Fuchs himself was suspected only through evidence picked up by chance in the United States. Moreover, we know that the Russians put certain queries to Fuchs—notably about the work

in Berkeley, California, and about the hydrogen bomb—queries
which were based on knowledge that could not have come to
them from any of the known traitors. It is therefore reasonable to assume that Fuchs and company were only part of the
network; how great a part of it nobody outside the Kremlin can
tell.

The next point—and this is the vital one—concerns the security
services. Could Fuchs and the other traitors have been kept out
of the atomic project? Could they have been detected long
before they actually were? Five days after the Fuchs trial
Mr. Attlee, then Prime Minister, made a statement to the House
of Commons, and since it is practically the only official statement on this subject that has been made in Britain it is worth
examining in some detail. He said:

I would like to say a word about a matter which has caused a
good deal of writing in the press—the Fuchs case. It is a most
deplorable and unfortunate incident. Here you have a refugee from
Nazi tyranny hospitably entertained who was secretly working against
the safety of this country. I say secretly because there is a great deal
of loose talk in the press suggesting inefficiency on the part of the
security services. I entirely deny that.

Not long after this man came into this country—that was in 1933—
it was stated that he was a Communist. The source of that information was the Gestapo. At that time the Gestapo accused everybody of
being Communists. When it was looked into there was no support for
it whatever. And from that time onwards there was no support. A
proper watch was kept at intervals. He is a brilliant scientist. He was
taken on in 1941 for special work by the Ministry of Aircraft Production, and was transferred to the Department for Scientific Research.
He went to America. He came back to Harwell. On all those occasions the proper enquiries were made, and there was nothing to be
brought against him. His intimate friends never had any suspicion.
The universities for which he worked had the highest opinion of his
work and of his character.

In the autumn of last year information came from the United States suggesting there had been some leakage while the British Mission, of which Fuchs was a member, was in the United States. This information did not point to any individual. The security service got to work with great energy and were, as the House knows, successful.

I take full responsibility for the efficiency of the security services, and I am satisfied that unless we had had the kind of secret police they have in totalitarian countries, and employed their methods, which are reprobated, rightly, by every one in this country, there were no means by which we could have found out about this man. I do not think there is anything that can cast the slightest slur on the security service; indeed, I think they acted promptly and effectively as soon as there was any line they could follow up. I do not think that any blame attaches either to the government of the right honourable gentleman opposite [Mr. Churchill, who was Prime Minister when Fuchs was first employed in atomic research], or to this government, or to any of the officials, for what occurred. I think we had here quite an extraordinary and exceptional case. I mention that because of the attacks which have been made.

It was a pity that no other facts about the Fuchs case were given at the time for Mr. Attlee's statement did not allay the uneasy feeling that the security services had been badly caught out, and that uneasiness has, if anything, increased since then. In North America it has been quite different. The public there has been very fully informed; indeed, ninety per cent of the information now available to the public about the atomic bomb, as well as about the atomic spies, has been released in the United States and Canada either in the form of government pamphlets or press conferences or in transcripts from Congressional hearings and the long and revealing trials of the American traitors. The American public has had every opportunity of learning about the activities of the FBI and the problems of security. In Britain, meanwhile, there have been only the two short trials of Nunn May and Fuchs, the single statement of Mr. Attlee quoted above, and the rest is silence. It is hardly surprising, then, that the case for British security has gone by default, and in the absence of any defence it has naturally been assumed that British security has been guilty of great inefficiency. Miss Rebecca West was moved to comment very trenchantly on Mr. Attlee's statement, in an article in the *Evening Standard* on June 4, 1951.

Now it is never wise [she wrote] for politicians to accuse journalists of loose talk. Which of these classes has done most of that will never be settled till the Day of Judgment, and no prudent person would bet more than half a crown on the result. But Mr. Attlee's talk was on that occasion superlatively loose, loose as Godiva's hair, loose as the folds of a hippopotamus's hide.

Miss West's main point is that the authorities must have known all along that Fuchs was a Communist, and if they did not know it then they should have done so, and in either case they failed to take the proper steps to keep Fuchs out of the atomic energy project. She suggests that Fuchs himself revealed that he was a Communist when he appeared before the Aliens Tribunal in Edinburgh in 1939.

Now in point of fact, as we have shown, Fuchs never made any such declaration to that Tribunal; he never revealed to any official in Britain or America that he was a Communist, until Skardon saw him at Harwell on December 21, 1949. In fact, throughout the whole of those ten years he made it his business to keep the matter a secret, and ten years is a long time in a man's life.

All the authorities had before them was that one report from the German Consul in Bristol, dated 1934. Now it is perfectly true that, had security between this date and the outbreak of war in 1939 cared to check with the Gestapo and ferret about among Fuchs' boyhood friends, they would have discovered that he had once been a Communist in Germany. But during this period there was no question of Fuchs doing any secret work, and security could not have taken this action until he was invited to join "Tube Alloys" in 1941. Then he could have been confronted only with the information from the Bristol Consul. What then? He answers you by taking an oath of allegiance to the British Crown. He signs a paper saying he will never divulge secrets to an unauthorised person. And in all his *known* actions, in everything he is observed to say and do, he is meticulously loyal and security-minded, even pedantically so.

What should you do in the face of this? Refuse to employ Fuchs, even though your need for him may be urgent—as it undoubtedly was from 1941 on, when he first joined "Tube Alloys"? Already then he had had nearly eight years' residence in England, with not one jot of evidence against him in that time. It may be true that after he arrived in England Fuchs continued to hold Communist views, and to associate privately with refugees and left-wing groups, but so did many other scientists in the United States as well as Britain and a number of them were employed on atomic energy projects. However one approaches the problem, one always comes back to the point that during the war our policy toward Communists was much more lenient than it is now, and it had every reason to be. After the war, when Russia's antagonism was apparent and our policy was changed, many of the Communists changed their views too. It was Britain's bad luck that she happened to sponsor men like Fuchs who remained implacable.

There are people who argue that a man who is once a Communist is always a Communist, but if that fallacious doctrine were acted on, then quite a number of high officials on both sides of the Atlantic would be promptly obliged to resign. The years bring changes in men's politics, and there was every evidence before the authorities that Fuchs, like so many others, had changed from a German refugee to a loyal British subject. The

authorities would have had no right whatever to refuse Fuchs
employment in 1941 on the grounds that he had been a Communist eight years before—even if they had known this. And,
in the absence of any further evidence against him, they had
every right to clear him to the Americans in 1943, and to admit
him to Harwell in 1946.

However, he was not accepted on trust at any stage of his
progress. There was a police investigation into his record when
he was first employed on atomic energy work in Birmingham
in 1941, and another investigation when he was naturalised in
1942. He was investigated a third time before he was sent to the
United States in 1943. Then he passed out of the surveillance of
British security for three years—at any rate as far as his physical
movements were concerned. Then, immediately he returns to
England in 1946 and enters Harwell, there is a fourth investigation, which goes on for months. None of these enquiries reveals
anything, and security in America has nothing to say against him
either.

But there still remains the question of security's watch on
Fuchs' actual movements. We know now that all this time Fuchs
was in fact seeing Russian agents. Why did security fail to observe him?

Now Fuchs himself has had a word to say on this point. He
said that as far as he can remember he never made a mistake.
He took the most elaborate precautions to make all his absences
seem casual and natural. He never talked politics, he never
slipped in any word he uttered among his friends. He had no
wife, and he had no confidant whatever.

If we add them up, we find he had perhaps a dozen meetings
in England before he went to America, four or five with Harry
Gold in New York, one meeting in Boston, two at Santa Fe,
and then another eight on his return to England in 1946; at the
outside some thirty meetings in all. Surely someone ought to

have caught him at one of these meetings.

There are several answers to this. Those thirty meetings were spread over seven years—an average of a little more than four meetings a year, and nearly all of them were in different places. Furthermore, except in one or two cases each meeting was short —perhaps a quarter of an hour or less. It seems a bit too much to expect of security that they should have been on guard during four separate quarter hours of a man's comings and goings scattered over twelve months. Unless they had special reason to suspect a man, such surveillance of the atomic scientists is manifestly absurd—it would require a vast army. Few people have any conception of just what is involved in the simple act of shadowing a man, even after he is suspected. If he is travelling by car along a country road he very soon becomes aware that a car is following him, and will not go to his rendezvous that day. If it is in the city—and most of these meetings were in the city—he sets out, let us say, from Paddington for the Mornington Crescent station by underground. He will not go direct to Mornington Crescent, but instead to Piccadilly Circus. Then, if you are successful in following him through the crowds, there you will find that he takes another train—again in the wrong direction. He will travel through three or four stations, and then at the last moment, when the train doors are closing, he will slip out. He will repeat this manoeuvre several times and if only one man is following him he will soon shake him off. So, not one, but perhaps ten or twenty men and women follow him, and they will drop off one by one as the hunt goes on. But even then it is nearly impossible to keep out of sight of an experienced agent— and Fuchs was not only experienced but meticulous about these matters.

There were tens of thousands of men employed on the atomic bomb project in the United States during the war, hundreds of whom knew as much as Fuchs did. American security did attach guards to the most senior people in the project (not to watch them so much as to protect them), and nobody blames American security for not including Fuchs in its list; he was not senior enough for that.

Mr. Gordon Dean, who was chairman of the United States Atomic Energy Commission at the time of the Fuchs case, gave a public interview in the form of questions and answers, and this interview throws a very revealing light indeed on Anglo-American security. It is worth quoting at some length:

Q. How long does it take to clear an individual?
A. The average today is 53 days.
Q. And also the money that it costs to do the clearing?
A. The cost is between $100 and $200 per person, and if you clear thousands of people for projects, that's a lot of money—and time.
Q. What percentage of people you examine fail to get clearance?
A. Very small. My guess is that it is less than half of one per cent.
Q. Would you say that the arrangement or setup you have with other governments for obtaining information from us is now satisfactory?
A. Do you mean, can we trust the certifications of other governments?
Q. Well, that is another way of putting it. The Fuchs case arose out of the fact that we didn't have it. Is the present arrangement satisfactory?
A. I think the present arrangement is generally satisfactory. We did have conferences, you know, with the British and the Canadian security officers immediately after this thing. They came over here and we had a three-day session, largely to determine the comparability of our security standards, and I think it is reasonably safe.
Q. You don't feel so apprehensive of losing out in that direction?
A. No, although in the most perfect system there may be someone who will slip through.

Q.   We now clear foreigners, don't we? We didn't clear Fuchs ourselves—we depended upon the British?

A.   You still can't have the F.B.I. running investigations through all
foreign countries, making their own investigations. What we have to do
is to delegate it to a competent security group, comparable to our
own, to make sure that the investigations cover the same types of
points we make here in the States. Of course, the F.B.I., in turn, does
the same thing for other governments. When someone is over here
that the foreign government wants to check on, the F.B.I. will make
the check for them.

Q.   Can you evaluate the damage that was done to our country by
Fuchs and his associates in terms of the Russian progress?

A.   It is hard to do, but I don't think you would be taking too
extreme a position if you said he had advanced them between a year
and two years.

Q.   To what extent did the British have access to our atomic information? I believe we were supposed to be partners with them in the
original development of atomic energy?

A.   During the War it was a complete partnership. The British
decided to give up trying on the gas-diffusion work and they came
over to this country and we had a complete partnership. As a matter
of fact there were about thirty, I believe, in the military mission from
Britain who went to Los Alamos. They knew everything. They helped
us very much in the development of the weapon. Since the War we
have operated under an understanding with the British and the
Canadians in several areas which are not weapon areas. We have
exchanged some visits within those areas, but that is the extent of it.

Q.   In weapons there is now no real exchange?

A.   No.

Q.   Has the Fuchs episode had any effect on those scientists who
were inclined for a long time to pooh-pooh the need for security—
American scientists who were a little bit annoyed and irritated by our
desire to have security, because they thought it was inconceivable that
Russia could do what she has done?

A.   I wouldn't limit it to scientists. I would say that the Fuchs episode has had a sobering effect upon everybody connected with the program.

Q. In that way it was a blessing in disguise?

A. I think so. Some good came of it. It certainly doesn't equal the bad, but some good did come of it.

Q. Have you any idea what is wrong with human beings or with our system in these democracies of ours that these people will do the things that Fuchs did? Does the scientist have less regard for loyalty to his country than other people? Is he a world citizen who wants to give everything away? What is the reason that Fuchs got into this thing?

A. I don't think you can say that scientists are an entirely different breed in that respect. In Fuchs' defence, let me say we have had some of them who were not scientists. Fuchs is the type of man who, while he might have been caught had there been a real security check on him, might never be caught by any kind of investigation, because apparently he owes his allegiance to nothing that ordinary humans owe theirs to. He is going to make his own decisions regardless of any rules he purports to operate under. What do you do with a man like that? Usually he is a very intelligent man. He is an independent man. He is an idealist of some kind. He might be a Communist idealist, but he is a man of ideals of some kind. You don't usually spot this type in a check.*

Although it is not quite clear what Mr. Dean means by "a real security check" in his last answer, it would be hard to find a fairer general statement of the case than this. Had this interview been given wider publicity, it would have done much to restore those Anglo-American relations which were befouled by Fuchs and Nunn May; and it would have gone some way toward rebutting the suggestion which is still everywhere prevalent that Fuchs would have been caught if only American security had not accepted the British clearance, but applied their own par-

* *Soviet Atomic Espionage*, U. S. Government Printing Office, Washington, 1951.

ticular methods to him. American security methods have failed just as the British have. There were other secret Communists besides Fuchs inside Los Alamos and they were American citizens who passed American clearance tests. Such traitors, as Mr. Dean says, are specialists of high intelligence, and no loyalty test is going to trip them up and no security system will infallibly detect the man who secretly changes his mind after he has already been investigated.

Now it is an entirely profitless business to go matching American Greenglasses and Golds against British Nunn Mays and Fuchses, or to try to compute which country has fathered the most traitors. As Miss West might say, this is an issue that will never be settled till the Day of Judgment and no prudent person would bet more than fifty cents on the result. The important thing is to realize that geographical boundaries and birthplaces have got very little to do with the matter: this is an international problem that concerns us all, and we have got to decide just how security can best operate in the United States, in Britain, and every other country in the West. Clearly the matter goes far beyond barbed wire, loyalty tests, steel safes, and special passes. It goes straight to the point which Mr. Alan Barth in his book *The Loyalty of Free Men* makes very well when he says:

Security is never absolute. . . . The Government of a free people must take certain chances for the sake of maintaining freedom which the government of a police state avoids because it holds freedom to be of no value.

If the Fuchses are the price we have to pay for freedom it might be argued that it would be much better not to be free. Let us, like Russia, immure ourselves and our secrets behind an iron curtain; let us set a police watch on the scientists, tap their telephone wires, and forbid their travel abroad. This might be an admirable method of security except that it would not work:

the Russians have had their traitors too, despite all the policing of their daily lives. Worse still, as the Nazis discovered to their undoing, the very imposition of such police restrictions drives good brains out of the country. To a great extent the atomic bomb was built by refugees who escaped from such oppression to England and America.

It would be absurd to suggest that Fuchs could not have been caught much earlier than he was. Clearly, if security had been a little more diligent, if they had more men and money, if they had been attended with a little more luck, and if the politics of the world had been different, they *could* have got him. But one wonders what sort of sentence he would have received if he had been caught at the time the Russians were fighting the Battle of Stalingrad. Certainly the public rage against him would have been far less. He might then have been regarded as no worse than a scientist who now passes atomic secrets between the United States and Britain. There is not much point, though, in pursuing that line of thought, and it cannot be seriously advanced in defence of the security system. In the end perhaps the case for security lies simply in this: Klaus Fuchs and the other traitors are something new in the world. They might have happened anywhere. And until there is some synthesis between Communism and democracy they might easily happen again.

Mr. Dean makes another useful point when he refuses to accept the idea that scientists as a class tend to be more disloyal than other people. The argument runs thus: scientists work in their laboratories by exact laws and, having little knowledge of the outside world, they think that politics as well should be conducted on exact laws. So Marx has a peculiar appeal for them. Furthermore, they are, by the very nature of their work, dependent on free enquiry, and are therefore apt to be internationalists.

There may be something in this. Yet there is no evidence that the scientists have produced more traitors than the other educated groups in the community. There have been diplomat traitors,* soldier traitors, politician traitors unending, and none of them had much to do with science. The scientist traitor has become so well known in the last decade only because he has had such sensational information to impart. Moreover, some confusion has existed in popular thought about the scientists. To be an internationalist is not, *ipso facto*, to be a traitor. Being the first to comprehend the destructive power they were creating, the atomic scientists very naturally were among the first to come forward and warn the world. They urged an international control, and a sharing of information, as the only feasible means of avoiding the possibility of an atomic war and unimaginable disasters for mankind. They have still to be proved wrong in this argument, and in any event, the fact that they put the argument forward does not turn them into traitors.

Sincerity is a marvellous disguise. It protected Fuchs. He took risks which no professional spy would have dreamed of taking. He was an internationalist in action—at least as far as Soviet Russia was concerned—and, wrapped up in that stupendous egotism, he walked through barbed wire like H. G. Wells' Invisible Man. In the end he was undone not by security (for that tip from the FBI in America by itself would never have caught him), but by something quite different: an attachment to the ordinary, simple values of life, when he finally settled down at Harwell. It would be naïve to press this point too far, and worse than naïve to suggest that he might not, under changed circumstances, have gone back to his treason. Yet one searches fruit-

* It should perhaps be noted here that Pontecorvo's disappearance had no connection in any way with the disappearance in 1951 of the two members of the British Foreign Office, Burgess and Maclean. The case of Burgess and Maclean is quite apart from that of the atomic traitors, except in so far as they too played their part—a drastic part—in undermining public confidence in the loyalty of officials.

lessly for any other explanation of his actions in 1949. He breaks contact with the Russians. He goes to the security officer and says, "I am a security risk, my father has gone over to the Russians," which was as good as saying, "Come and get me, I have something to confess. I want above all else to stay on here at Harwell, but I can't do it until this thing is purged."

He reiterates again and again throughout his investigation his fear that his friends will never be got to understand—he has damaged them too much. He repeats the same thought in his confession to Skardon, and he ends up with, "Since coming to Harwell I have met English people of all kinds, and I have come to see in many of them a deep-rooted firmness which enables them to lead a decent way of life. I do not know where this springs from, and I don't think they do; but it is there." And finally, on his arrest, he has just one thing to say: "You realise what this will mean at Harwell?

It all reads like some crude and too easy moral tale in an improving book for children; the wolf draws in his fangs and repents at last because somebody has been kind to him. Yet it is not unknown, in moments of crisis and confession, for the truth to be discovered in obvious and simple places. Through the most impressionable part of his life Fuchs had no social background to act as a compensation for his private dreams of power and glory. He was conscious, like so many other men of talent, of his own abilities, but he had to take a back seat as a refugee student in England. Treason was a wonderful way of demonstrating his powers, and there was no family and no close circle of friends to bring him back to his senses by the mere fact of their being there and having affection for him. But at Harwell he is an established man, the head of a department. His powers are recognised. He is comfortable and respected. There is no longer any need for the secret compensation of his treason. So he lies in bed agonising over the problem of how to kill his past and make his home here, safe and secure, among his friends. He wants to attach himself to a tradition at last, to achieve that feeling of security that comes only from living in a community that has been settled for a long time in one place.

It may be that one approach to the whole complicated problem of loyalty lies here: that it can be guaranteed only by tradition, by fixed habits, by a long period of freedom from fear, and by affection. And all this must be backed by a philosophy, or a religion, or at any rate some kind of faith which is rather stronger than the democracies have yet been able to engender. A fear of Russia in itself hardly amounts to a faith. There has to be something on the positive side, an ideal of some kind. The crime of the Fuchses and the Nunn Mays was that they concentrated upon what they believed to be an ideal, and lost their affection for the ordinary, fallible human beings around them. They lost their humility, and when that was gone, they lost their judgment too. They imagined they could do without the affection of their friends. Perhaps, in the end, in their own way, they all came to see they were wrong in this. Perhaps Marianne Pontecorvo saw it when she broke down and cried on leaving England. Perhaps Fuchs saw it at last when he said, "You realise what this will mean at Harwell?"

This book has no practical, ready-made solution of the security problem to offer. Perhaps something more might be done, in future, to check the family backgrounds of the men employed on atomic projects. In Britain loyalty tests are not liked, partly because it is felt that they discover nothing, and partly because it is felt that they destroy something of the tradition of freedom on which loyalty itself is based. But in America there are other methods—notably the "compartmentalisation" of scientists, so that any one man knows only a part of the pattern—that might well be more fully explored. (But this method achieved no success in the U.S.A. in the case of Fuchs.) Certainly in Britain a much franker and fuller public discussion of the traitors, and the whole problem of security, would be a healthy thing. But none of these points provides a complete answer: the complete answer does not exist. The eternal equation continues: the greater the prosperity of a democracy, the smaller the revolutionary Communist Party; the greater the absence of fear, the fewer the traitors.

In the ideal state, which is perfectly prosperous and secure, the only threat that can come is from the anarchist, the man who glories in chaos and change for its own sake, and it has yet to be proved that any of the atomic traitors are anarchists. Nor is their treason to be confused with the legend of Faust or with Robert Louis Stevenson's Doctor Jekyll; Faust and Jekyll thirsted purely after knowledge and power. They so believed in the right and in the necessity of man to obtain knowledge that they were quite prepared to break all bonds of loyalty and destroy society in the process. So they were anarchists of a sort. These scientists were quite different. Every sane nuclear physicist of the 20th century (and this includes the traitors) has urged that, if we can get all nations to agree, we should seal up our knowledge of atomic weapons forthwith, that we should make no further enquiries in that direction but devote ourselves wholly to the exploration of useful and harmless atomic energy.

Whatever his turgid loyalties may have been, Fuchs was a responsible man—he did nothing lightly. He projected, perhaps more than anybody else, one of the major problems of the mid-20th century, and one of its worst agonies—the problem of the scientist who goes on and on into the physical world, making one discovery after another, until at length he becomes a creator, and a destroyer, in his own right, and somewhere in this journey he loses his faith. He looks back over his shoulder, as it were, searching for some ethic, some system of law and order, on which to base his discoveries, and he finds nothing solid. Here is the atomic power with infinite capabilities for good or evil, but where are the morals to govern it? Somehow a system of government has got to be found and quickly, while there is still time.

A preoccupation with this problem is not peculiar to Fuchs. Most serious atomic scientists, as we have said, have been acutely concerned with it. Though only a few of them selected Marxist ethics as the right basis for atomic power, and still fewer turned themselves into men of action in the Marxist faith, nearly all of them, at some time, have believed that the only hope for the world was for all men to share this secret, and having shared it, to shun it like the plague.

The real charge against Fuchs is that of impudence. He rushed in and took the whole problem on his own shoulders. He knew less than most men about human nature, he had never been to Russia, he had no experience of diplomacy or political administration, he was an atheist, yet he still judged himself competent to put the world to rights. Mr. Alan Barth makes a point about the Fuchses of this world. Describing another traitor—an American—in his book, he says he had

a kind of idealism, however mistaken and misplaced. The sense that because "something drastic had to be done" he, personally, had to do it, is a sense out of which saints as well as sinners, great patriots as well as base traitors, are made.

Possibly, as Mr. Barth suggests when he quotes the letters of the younger Pliny to the Emperor Trajan about A.D. 112, you have to go back to the early Christians to find any sort of parallel for the atomic traitors. Describing his method of dealing with the Christians, Pliny says:

I asked them if they were Christians. If they admitted it I asked them a second and again a third time, adding threats of death. If they still claimed to be Christians, I gave orders for their execution. . . .

Soon in the usual way the investigation itself led to further accusations, covering several types of charge. An anonymous accusation
appeared, containing many names. Some of those named denied that
they were Christians or ever had been. As they joined with me in
invocations to the gods and offered supplications with incense and
wine to your Majesty's ikon, which I had brought in with the divine
images for this purpose, and finally cursed Christ, I thought they
could be discharged, as it is said that genuine Christians cannot be
forced into these acts. Others whose names were quoted by the in-
former said they were Christians but soon withdrew their plea; to be
sure they had once been Christians, but they had ceased, some three
years before, some for a longer time and a few even for twenty-five
years. All these worshipped your Majesty's ikon and the images of the
gods; and cursed Christ.*

Trajan approved these practises, but he warned Pliny that he
should have nothing to do with anonymous accusations; they
were thoroughly bad and out of keeping with the spirit of the
age. This was a humane and statesmanlike approach, but
the end result of it was that the Roman gods vanished and the
Christians survived and multiplied. Neither Trajan nor Pliny
apparently was confronted with the kind of man who would
curse Christ in public while he continued to worship him in
private. It was left to the Communists to perfect that kind of
double life. Nor had the Christians the secret of great physical
power, as the atomic traitors had. Still, the seat of treason in
each case is the same: the inner conviction of the accused that
what he is doing is right. The Christians were moved by their
faith in God, while Fuchs acted upon his megalomaniac confidence in his own brain, but both were so convinced of their
rightness that they were prepared to destroy the state in order
to have their way.

Perhaps Fuchs was telling the truth when he claimed after

* The Rise of Christianity, R. W. Barnes, Longmans, Green Co., Inc., 1947.

his arrest that his loyalties were now fixed in England, and his public cursing of Russian Marxism was sincere. But he was basically a man who would always refer to his own conscience first and society afterward. There is no place for such men in an ordered community.

But the problem they have propounded—what to do with atomic power before it destroys us all, and how to guarantee the loyalties of men's minds in the use of that power—that problem still remains.

Sources

•

1. *The Report of the Royal Commission*, appointed by the Canadian Government in February 1946, to investigate the facts relating to and surrounding the communication, by public officials and other persons in positions of trust, of secret and confidential information, to agents of a foreign power.

2. *Soviet Atomic Espionage*, printed for the use of the Joint Committee on Atomic Energy by the United States Government Printing Office, Washington, 1951.

3. *Atomic Energy*, by H. D. Smyth, the United States Government Printing Office, 1945.

4. *The Atomic Age. The Halley Stewart Lectures*, 1948. Allen & Unwin, London, 1949.

5. *Atomic Energy*, Royal Institute of International Affairs, 1948.

6. *Christ in Catastrophe*, by Doctor Emil Fuchs, published by the Friends Home Service Committee, and other pamphlets by Doctor Fuchs.

7. *The Crime of the Century*, by J. Edgar Hoover, *The Reader's Digest*, June 1951.

8. Hansard, 1946–1951.

Verbatim reports of the trials of Allan Nunn May at the Old Bailey on May 1, 1946, and of Klaus Fuchs on March 1, 1950.

Index

•

Wells, H. G.
  The Invisible Man, 219
  The *Outline of History*, 52
Wells Survey, Inc., 185
West, Rebecca, 217
  quoted on Fuchs, 171-72
  quoted on security, 210
Whitehead, Detective Inspector William, 38

Willkie, Wendell, 40
Windscale, England (site of plutonium pile), 120
World War II, 77-79

Yakovlev, Anatoli A., 98, 99
Young Communist League, 28

Zabotin, Colonel, 3, 5-7, 21, 27, 29, 30, 35, 39

Format by Katharine Sitterly
Set in Linotype Caledonia
Composed, printed and bound by The Haddon Craftsmen, Inc.
HARPER & ROW, PUBLISHERS, INCORPORATED